The World on Credit:
1772, The First Credit Panic

THE WORLD ON CREDIT is a **Xenoloop** Publishing House series.

By **Xenoloop Editorial Collective**

Series created and curated by **Dr. Vignesh K**

Title: The World on Credit
Subtitle: 1772: The First Credit Panic
Author: Xenoloop Editorial Collective created by Dr. Vignesh K
Publisher: Xenoloop Publishing House

ISBN Paperback: 978-81-988896-2-1

DECLARATION

A Note on History, Fiction, and Method

This volume is a historically inspired narrative built on the documented events of the 1772–1773 credit crisis and its ripple effects across Britain and Europe.

To make complex financial mechanics readable and cinematic, this book uses:

Fictional and composite characters to represent real roles (clerks, merchants, bankers, and officials).

Invented private conversations and scene details to dramatize plausible human decisions inside a real macro event.

The core crisis structure, its trigger, escalation, and spread, is based on history. The storytelling approach is designed to bring the lived experience of a financial panic onto the page.

CONTENTS

	PREFACE	vii
1	PAPER IS FASTER THAN GOLD	Pg 1
2	THE BET AGAINST AN EMPIRE	Pg 13
3	THREADNEEDLE STREET SMILES	Pg 28
4	8TH JUNE	Pg 43
5	BLACK MONDAY	Pg 60
6	HORSEMAN TO EDINBURGH	Pg 74
7	LAND IS NOT LIQUIDITY	Pg 86
8	AMSTERDAM FREEZES	Pg 100
9	WHO GETS SAVED?	Pg 112
10	THE WORLD ON CREDIT	Pg 125

PREFACE

This book is written to be read like a serious, cinematic story, because the truth is that financial crises are not abstract. They happen through people, rooms, documents, delays, and decisions made under pressure.

You may know The World on Credit from my earlier self-published nonfiction work focused on the 2008 financial crisis and related modern financial themes. This volume is not a conventional "revised and expanded" edition of that book. Instead, it is a relaunch of the title as a series brand, under Xenoloop Publishing House, with a different narrative method and a wider historical scope.

Here is the transparent reason for the change:

The earlier book explained crises through analysis.

This series aims to explain crises through experience, so readers can feel how confidence breaks, how panic spreads, and how institutions react when the system is tested.

To do that, this volume uses a technique often called narrative history or documentary-style thriller writing:

- Real macro events as the spine
- Clear scenes and human viewpoints to carry the reader
- Financial mechanisms shown through actions (queues, settlements, letters, bank rooms), not lectures
- Short moments of explanation only when they unlock what the characters are facing

If you want reference points for this style, books that demonstrate how complex realities can be turned into gripping narrative include:

The Big Short (Michael Lewis) — systems explained through people and structure

The Devil in the White City (Erik Larson) — history told with novel-like momentum

Say Nothing (Patrick Radden Keefe) — investigative history with thriller pacing

This first series volume begins in 1772 because it is one of the earliest moments where the modern credit machine becomes visible: paper promises move faster than gold, confidence becomes the real currency, and the collapse spreads beyond a single city.

Finally, one important note: while this series uses narrative techniques, our intent is not to blur truth. The book includes a clear declaration of what is historical and what is fictionalized for storytelling. The goal is clarity, not confusion.

Welcome to the beginning of The World on Credit.

— Dr. Vignesh K
Series Creator & Curator, Xenoloop Publishing House

ABOUT XENOLOOP EDITORIAL COLLECTIVE

The Xenoloop Editorial Collective develops cinematic, research-led books that translate complex realities into readable stories. Our work combines historical grounding with narrative craft, designed for readers who want clarity without dryness—and stories with real-world weight.

Xenoloop Publishing House

CHAPTER 1

PAPER IS FASTER THAN GOLD

London always smells like a promise.

Not the clean, honest kind. In a kind of bread in the oven, rain on stone. London's promise is ink, sweat, and coal smoke. It creeps under doors. It sticks to collars. It lives in the folds of ledgers and the pause between a people's words when she or he says, *I will pay*.

The morning AJ Sen arrived on Lombard Street, the city had the polished calm of something that had not yet been asked the wrong question.

The carriage dropped him at the edge of a narrow lane and rolled away, as if even the wheels wanted distance from the work that happened here. The buildings leaned in. The air was busy with footsteps, with parchment, with men who knew how to keep their faces still.

AJ stood for a moment and looked up at the sign above the door:

NEAL, JAMES, FORDYCE & DOWN
Bankers and Merchants

The letters were gold leaf. The kind of gold that didn't buy food. The kind that told the world: *We are safe*.

He pressed his palm against the leather satchel strapped across his chest, feeling the reassuring rectangle of his appointment letter. His mother had called it a blessing. His father had called it a leash.

AJ called it, quietly, to himself, the edge of a life he could not see beyond.

He adjusted his cuffs, tucked his chin, and entered.

Inside, the bank held its breath.

Not from fear but from discipline. Everything here was measured, controlled, arranged into rectangles: the dark wood counters, the iron grilles, the lines of clerks at their desks, heads bent like monks over scripture.

A bell rang once, small and sharp.

A man in a coat too well-cut for work and too plain for vanity glided toward him. His hair was powdered without flourish; his face held the patient irritation of someone who had become successful by never being surprised.

"Arjun Sen?" the man asked, as if the name were a coin he was weighing.

"Yes, sir."

"Mr. Harrington. Chief clerk." A brief glance. Not unkind. Not welcoming either. "You're early."

"I didn't want to be late."

"That is the correct instinct." Harrington turned and motioned. "Come."

AJ followed him into a corridor lined with closed doors and quiet power. Names were painted in small lettering: partners, managers, legal counsel. Each door a mouth that could swallow a man.

They reached a room at the back. It was not large, but it was heavy: heavy with shelves of bound volumes, heavy with the smell of wax and old paper. A single tall window let in winter light that seemed reluctant to enter.

In the center stood a desk that looked like it belonged to the building.

Harrington placed AJ's letter on the table without reading it, as if words were less important than the fact that it existed.

"Your hand?" he asked.

"My hand?"

"Your writing."

AJ paused. "Neat."

Harrington's eyes flicked up. "Fast?"

"Yes."

"Silent?"

AJ swallowed. "Yes."

"Good." Harrington's voice softened by half a grain, the way a man might soften for a tool he approves of. "You will sit at the third row, near the ledger cabinet. You will copy figures and correspondence. You will not correct your superiors unless asked. You will not invent answers. You will not improvise with other people's money."

"I understand."

Harrington leaned closer—just close enough that AJ could smell the faint bite of snuff.

"And you will learn something today," he said. "If you're not a fool."

AJ's pulse jumped. "Sir?"

Harrington straightened. "Follow."

They returned to the main hall, passing desks where quills moved like insects. Clerks murmured numbers to themselves under their breath, lips barely moving, as though speaking them aloud might summon consequences.

Clients stood at the counter. Men in fine coats and men in worn coats. A widow in black. A young man with the damp shine of desperation in his eyes. Respectable faces, anxious hands.

Harrington didn't stop at the front counter. He led AJ deeper—past the obvious business and into the place where the bank kept its secret.

They reached an iron gate. Harrington produced a key and opened it.

Beyond was a chamber that smelled different—colder, mineral. The air was the kind that makes you aware of your own breath.

A vault door sat in the wall like an accusation.

Harrington turned the wheel slowly. Metal groaned. A sound like something ancient being disturbed.

When the door swung open, AJ saw the heart of the bank.

Gold, yes. Stacked coins in neat cylinders. Bars that looked too heavy to be real. A row of canvas sacks tied at the mouth like restrained animals.

But what struck him wasn't the gold.

It was how little of it there was.

AJ had never held the fantasies of merchants and gentlemen close to his chest, but even he had expected more. A bank, he thought, would be a cave of treasure.

This was… contained. Managed. Not poor, not rich. *Finite.*

Harrington watched him read the room.

"This," Harrington said, voice low, "is what people think we are."

He shut the vault door again, with more care than ceremony, and locked it.

Then he led AJ to another cabinet along the wall, this one made of wood, filled with paper.

Folders. Bundles. Sealed envelopes. Sheets of parchment stacked higher than any gold.

Harrington pulled out a sheaf and handed it to AJ.

AJ took it carefully. The paper was thick. The ink was clean. The writing was elegant.

At the bottom, a signature, and beneath it a wax seal.

"What is it?" AJ asked.

"A bill of exchange," Harrington said. "A promise."

He pulled out another. And another. And another. He stacked them in AJ's arms until AJ's elbows ached under the weight.

"These are not gold," Harrington said. "And yet they buy ships. They buy sugar. They buy time. They buy power."

AJ looked down at the stack, stunned by how heavy a promise could become when you piled enough of them together.

"How?" he asked, because the question rose in him like a cough.

Harrington smiled—not warmly. The smile of a man who knows the trick and never wants the audience to fully understand it.

"Because everyone agrees to pretend," he said. "Because everyone agrees the signature means something. Because men fear being the first to doubt."

He took the bills back, returned them, and shut the cabinet.

"There," Harrington continued, "is the true vault."

He tapped the wood with his knuckle. *Knock-knock*. Like a man checking the wall of a prison.

"Paper is faster than gold," he said. "Paper travels where metal cannot. Paper multiplies. Paper—"

He paused and looked AJ in the eyes.

"—paper kills," he finished softly, as if he were speaking of a disease.

A bell rang again in the main hall. Two quick rings. A signal.

Harrington stiffened. "Stay behind me."

They returned to the hall, and AJ felt the difference immediately.

Something had shifted.

Not chaos. Not yet. But a tightening. The quiet had sharpened. Voices were lower. Clerks glanced up more often. A man at the counter was speaking too quickly, pressing his hands flat on the wood as if trying to push his demand through it.

"I want it withdrawn," the man said. "Today. In coin."

"Sir," the cashier replied, calm with effort, "your funds can be provided, but—"

"But what? It is my money."

"It is your deposit," the cashier said carefully.

"It is my money," the man repeated, louder this time, and the last syllable cracked like a whip.

Harrington strode forward, interposing himself with the practiced ease of someone whose body was trained to block trouble.

"Mr. Wray," he said, recognizing the man. "Good morning."

The man's eyes darted. "Harrington. Yes. Good morning. Tell your man to stop speaking in circles."

Harrington's smile was an instrument. "We're not circling. We're ensuring you receive what you want in the most secure manner."

"I want coin."

"Of course."

Mr. Wray leaned in. He smelled of wet wool and worry. "I heard something."

There it was. The sentence that had ended more fortunes than any war.

"I heard," Mr. Wray said again, "that some houses are… strained."

Harrington's expression did not change. "Rumors are a cheap currency, sir."

Mr. Wray swallowed. "Is it a rumor about *this* house?"

Harrington's eyes held his. "This house has been standing longer than you've been trading."

Mr. Wray's jaw worked as if chewing a thought. "Then why is everyone withdrawing?"

"No one is everyone," Harrington said. "And the city always gets nervous when the East India Company coughs."

At that, Mr. Wray flinched. The East India Company: the empire's fat heart, pumping profits and poison across oceans.

AJ felt his chest tighten.

"Provide the coin," Mr. Wray insisted, voice dipping into embarrassment. "I'll sleep better."

Harrington nodded. "Of course. Please, take a seat."

Mr. Wray moved to the side, as if he had won.

But AJ saw what had happened.

Harrington had not refused. He had not fought. He had soothed.

Because the bank's power was not in saying no.

It was in keeping the man calm enough to keep pretending.

Harrington turned his head slightly. "Sen," he said without looking at him.

"Yes, sir?"

"Come." Harrington walked toward the desks. "This is your seat."

AJ sat at the third row. A narrow desk. An inkwell. A quill. A ruled sheet waiting like an open mouth.

Harrington placed a thick ledger in front of him. The cover was worn, edges darkened by hands. The spine creaked as if reluctant to reveal what it contained.

"This," Harrington said, "is a book of deposits."

AJ traced the title with his eyes. The ink had bled slightly over years. Names. Figures.

Each line looked like a small, polite fact.

But AJ could feel the truth underneath: these were not just numbers.

These were lives.

Harrington bent and pointed with a finger—clean nail, ink-stained skin.

"Here," he said. "You will copy this page into the new register. You will not make errors."

"I won't."

Harrington's finger moved down the list, stopping at a name.

AJ read it:

FORDYCE, ALEXANDER — £—

The figure was too large. His mind refused to hold it at once.

"Sir," AJ said, and his voice betrayed him with the slightest tremor, "is that—"

Harrington snapped the ledger shut.

The sound was not loud, but it silenced AJ as effectively as a slap.

"You will learn," Harrington said, "what questions to ask—and when."

AJ lowered his eyes. "Yes, sir."

Harrington straightened, smoothing his cuffs, as if restoring order to his own body.

"Work," he said simply.

He walked away.

AJ dipped the quill and began.

He copied the names. The pounds. The shillings. The pence. He copied until the numbers began to hum in his skull, until the ink smelled like something he'd eaten.

And while he wrote, the bank continued its rituals: the whispered conversations, the polite firmness, the occasional tightening of a clerk's jaw.

Hours passed.

Then, near midday, the main doors opened and a man entered whose presence changed the air without a word.

He was not tall, but he moved as if the building belonged to him. His coat was a shade richer than the others, his hat carried in his hand instead of worn. He smiled too easily. He looked at people as if he liked what he saw—and expected them to like him back.

Behind him, two men followed—one carrying a portfolio, the other wearing the kind of expression that comes from worrying in private for a powerful friend.

Harrington appeared at once, as if summoned by gravity.

"Mr. Fordyce," Harrington said.

So this was him.

Alexander Fordyce.

The name that had made Mr. Wray's voice crack.

Fordyce's smile widened. "Harrington. You're as punctual as a sermon."

Harrington bowed his head slightly. Respect. Not affection.

Fordyce's gaze drifted across the hall, and for an instant it touched AJ.

AJ froze, quill hovering.

Fordyce's eyes were bright. Neither kind nor cruel. *Sharp.* The eyes of someone who saw the invisible lines between people, the debts, the favors, the leverage.

Fordyce's lips curled. A private amusement.

Then he looked away, and AJ exhaled.

Fordyce walked toward the partner doors. Harrington kept pace. The two men behind them followed like shadows.

As Fordyce passed, AJ caught a phrase—just a fragment—spoken low, meant for Harrington alone.

"—EIC's overvalued," Fordyce said, voice smooth as polished wood. "The market's drunk on empire."

Harrington's reply was too quiet to hear.

Fordyce laughed softly. "I'm not afraid to short a god."

They disappeared into the back.

AJ sat still, quill dripping a single black bead onto the page like a drop of blood.

Short a god.

He didn't know all the mechanics yet. He wasn't meant to. But he understood enough to feel the shape of danger.

A bank was a story people told themselves.

A merchant's wealth was a story.

An empire was a story.

And the most dangerous men were the ones who thought they could rewrite the ending.

AJ wiped the ink blot with the edge of his sleeve, but the stain spread instead, blooming into a bruise.

He stared at it.

In the stain, he saw something he couldn't name yet.

Not fear exactly.

More like the awareness that a room can be warm and still be on fire.

He opened the ledger again, slowly, as if it might bite.

His eyes found Fordyce's line.

The figure sat there, calm and arrogant, a mountain made of ink.

AJ looked across the hall.

At the clients.

At the widow's clasped hands.

At Mr. Wray, still seated, watching the counter like a man watching a doctor.

At the clerks bent over their pages as if worshiping.

Then AJ looked back down.

His quill hovered above the paper.

And for the first time in his life, he realized something that made his stomach go cold:

A number could be true and still be a lie.

He set the quill down.

He listened.

The bank's quiet had changed again, barely. A rustle. A shiver traveling desk to desk.

A messenger had entered, breathless, mud on his boots, a sealed note in his hand.

He moved fast, straight toward the back doors.

Harrington intercepted him and took the note without ceremony.

Harrington broke the seal.

Read.

His face didn't change.

But his fingers tightened on the paper until the parchment creased.

He turned and looked out across the hall.

For a brief moment, his gaze met AJ's.

And AJ understood, without knowing why, that something had just begun.

Not later.

Not tomorrow.

Now.

Harrington folded the note and tucked it inside his coat.

Then he raised his voice, calm, measured, like a man announcing a prayer.

"Gentlemen," he said, "continue your work."

The clerks bent lower.

The pens moved faster.

The ink kept flowing.

But the air had shifted for good.

AJ picked up his quill again.

He wrote.

And outside, somewhere beyond Lombard Street, beyond the vault of gold and the vault of paper, the city carried on,

unaware that its most fragile currency was no longer money.

It was faith.

CHAPTER 2

THE BET AGAINST AN EMPIRE

The city did not sleep.

It merely changed costumes.

By evening, Lombard Street's hard faces softened into silk and laughter. The same men who argued over half-percents at noon now leaned into candlelight as if it could forgive them. The same hands that signed promissory notes now lifted glasses—wine dark as ink, brandy bright as fire.

AJ left the bank late, his fingers cramped from copying columns that refused to end. He walked out with the other clerks, swallowed by the stream of bodies, pushed along by the city's night current.

Harrington had dismissed them in the same calm voice, but the calm had been forced—like a lid held down on boiling water.

Gentlemen, continue your work.

A sentence meant to keep a world intact.

AJ reached the boarding house where he rented a small room above a baker's shop. The stairs smelled of flour and damp wood. He ate quickly—stale bread, cheese—and sat at the narrow table by his window, trying to read by the thin light of a candle.

But his eyes kept returning to the same image:

Harrington breaking the seal.

Reading.

His fingers tightening.

A room changing without anyone daring to name it.

AJ closed the book and stared at the candle flame until it made a ghost of itself on his vision.

Then he heard it.

A knock at the door.

Not the careless knock of a neighbor.

A deliberate one. Two taps. Pause. One more.

AJ's throat tightened. He stood, crossed the room, and opened the door.

A man in a dark coat stood in the corridor. He was not a clerk. His boots were too clean, his hat too good. He carried a portfolio under one arm like it weighed nothing.

"Arjun Sen?" the man asked, quiet and precise.

"Yes."

The man's gaze flicked past AJ's shoulder into the room—taking in the cheap furniture, the thin blanket, the single candle. A survey. A measurement.

"I'm Mr. Lark," he said. "From the bank."

AJ's stomach dropped.

"I—did I make an error?" he asked at once.

Lark's mouth softened into something almost amused. "If you had, I wouldn't have come personally."

He extended a folded card. Heavy paper, clean edges. A name pressed into it.

MR. ALEXANDER FORDYCE
Requests the pleasure of your attendance
This evening, nine o'clock
At the Crown & Anchor, Strand

AJ stared at it. The letters seemed to lift off the card like heat.

"Mr. Fordyce?" AJ managed.

Lark nodded. "You were noticed."

"By him?"

"By someone close enough to him to matter," Lark corrected. Then, after a beat: "Wear your best coat."

"I—sir, I'm only a clerk."

Lark's eyes sharpened. "Exactly."

He turned and walked away without another word, leaving AJ holding the card as if it might burn through his skin.

For a long moment AJ stood in the doorway, listening to Lark's footsteps fade down the stairs.

Then he shut the door carefully, slid the bolt into place, and stared at the invitation again.

His pulse thudded in his ears.

This was not normal.

A partner did not summon a junior clerk to a fashionable tavern unless he wanted something that required a clerk's hands and a clerk's silence.

AJ washed his face with cold water from the basin. The water bit into his cheeks. He combed his hair until it lay obediently. He put on the least-worn coat he owned, the one he'd bought for his interview, and stood in front of the small mirror.

A thin young man looked back, neat, intelligent, careful. The kind of man who survived by disappearing into other people's shadows.

Tonight, he would be placed under a brighter light.

He blew out the candle and left.

The Crown & Anchor was not a tavern.

It was a stage.

The doorway alone announced wealth: polished brass, a doorman who looked at you as if your bones contained your social value. Inside, the air was warm with smoke and perfume and roasted meat. Voices collided in the space like billiard balls, laughter sharp as cutlery.

AJ's boots felt too loud on the floor.

He hesitated, uncertain where to go, until a waiter approached as if he'd been waiting for him.

"Mr. Sen?" the waiter asked.

AJ nodded.

"This way, sir."

He was led through the main hall, past rooms where men argued over cards and women laughed as if laughing were a profession. Past a curtained doorway guarded by another man in a coat too fine for work.

The guard looked AJ over, then lifted the curtain.

AJ stepped through.

And the noise dimmed, as if the room itself was lined with money.

A private chamber: dark wood, golden candlelight, a table laid with silver. There were only six men inside, and yet AJ felt as if he had entered a room crowded with invisible power.

Alexander Fordyce stood near the fireplace, a glass in his hand, laughing at something one of the others had said.

Up close, Fordyce was even more dangerous than he'd seemed in the bank.

He had the ease of a man who never doubted his own place in the world. His face was handsome without being gentle. His eyes were alive—too alive—like a gambler's eyes, always calculating what the next moment could be made to yield.

When Fordyce saw AJ, his smile stopped being general and became specific.

"Ah," Fordyce said, as if he'd been expecting a particular instrument and it had finally arrived. "Mr. Sen."

AJ bowed awkwardly. "Sir."

Fordyce crossed the room and took AJ's hand as though AJ were an equal. His grip was firm, warm, almost intimate.

"New to our house," Fordyce said. "And already you look like a man who can keep his mouth shut."

"I—yes, sir."

Fordyce laughed softly. "Good answer."

He guided AJ to the table with a hand at AJ's elbow, a gesture that felt friendly and controlling at once.

"Gentlemen," Fordyce said, addressing the room, "this is Arjun Sen. One of Harrington's fresh quills."

The men turned to look at AJ.

One was older, red-faced, with a banker's heavy jowls and the restless eyes of a man who feared losing what he had.

Another was slim, aristocratic, wearing boredom like a medal.

A third, younger than the others, wore rings and smelled of expensive tobacco. His smile was quick and thin.

A fourth sat in the shadow near the window, almost still, eyes bright as pins.

They looked at AJ not with contempt, but with a kind of appraisal.

Like one might look at a new lock and wonder which key it took.

Fordyce poured AJ a drink without asking. Dark amber, strong.

"Drink," Fordyce said. "It will steady your nerves and loosen your imagination. Both are useful."

AJ lifted the glass and drank. The liquid burned a line down his throat, and warmth spread in his chest.

Fordyce watched him swallow, satisfied.

"Tell me," Fordyce said, "what do you think we do all day in that hall of grim faces?"

AJ hesitated. "We… manage deposits. Provide loans. Facilitate trade."

Fordyce nodded. “A clerk’s answer.”

The aristocratic man chuckled into his glass.

Fordyce leaned closer. “I’ll tell you what we do,” he said. “We manufacture tomorrow.”

He stepped back and spread his hands as if presenting an artwork.

“We take a man’s future earnings and let him spend them today,” Fordyce continued. “We take a merchant’s cargo that is still weeks from port and allow him to sell it now. We take the invisible and make it negotiable.”

The younger man with rings smiled. “A miracle, really.”

Fordyce’s eyes flashed. “Exactly. A miracle. And like all miracles, it only works if people believe.”

AJ sat very still, feeling the room close around him.

The older banker grunted. “Belief is a delicate thing these days.”

Fordyce’s smile sharpened. “Belief is always delicate. That’s why it is profitable.”

He glanced at AJ. “Do you know what the East India Company is worth?”

AJ’s mouth went dry. “It… it’s enormous.”

Fordyce laughed. “A boyish answer, but true.”

He turned, and with a flick of his wrist he drew a folded paper from his coat—an extract from a newspaper or a broker’s list. He laid it on the table.

“Look,” Fordyce said.

AJ leaned in. Stock prices. Columns. Numbers marching like soldiers. And there it was, like a throne in ink:

EAST INDIA COMPANY

Fordyce tapped it with one finger.

“This,” he said softly, “is where the city is drunk.”

The aristocratic man sighed. "It's the empire itself. Everyone wants a share."

The older banker rubbed his temple. "It pays. It always pays."

Fordyce's gaze narrowed. "Does it?" he asked. "Or do we merely agree to say it does, because the alternative is too ugly to imagine?"

The man with rings leaned forward, interested. "Are you saying it's weak?"

Fordyce smiled like a man about to tell a secret.

"I'm saying it's overpraised," he said. "Overvalued. Bloated with confidence."

AJ felt his palms turn damp.

Fordyce lowered his voice slightly—enough to make everyone lean in.

"I'm saying the Company's stock is a temple built on paper," he said. "And I've decided to test whether it has stone beneath."

The younger man with rings inhaled. "You're shorting it."

Fordyce's smile widened as if he'd been complimented.

"Yes," he said. "I'm shorting it."

AJ had heard the term that day in the bank, but hearing it spoken here—casually, like a joke—made it feel like a blade.

The older banker muttered, "Madness."

Fordyce looked at him with affectionate contempt. "Courage," he corrected. "Or perhaps clarity."

He lifted his glass. "To clarity."

The others raised theirs, some eagerly, some reluctantly.

AJ raised his glass late, imitating them.

"Now," Fordyce said, turning back to AJ, "tell me what happens when a man shorts."

AJ hesitated. "He… borrows shares, sells them, and hopes to buy them back later at a lower price. The difference is profit."

Fordyce's eyes brightened. "Good," he said. "You can think."

He circled the table slowly, like a director arranging actors.

"And what happens if the price rises?" Fordyce asked, voice velvet.

AJ swallowed. "He loses."

"How much?"

AJ's mind raced. "Potentially… unlimited."

Fordyce stopped behind AJ's chair and leaned down, speaking near his ear.

"Unlimited," he repeated softly, savoring the word.

AJ felt the hair at the back of his neck lift.

The aristocratic man chuckled. "He likes the danger."

Fordyce straightened. "I like truth," he said, as if danger and truth were the same.

He returned to his place by the fireplace.

"But here is the finer point," Fordyce continued. "The city thinks the Company is untouchable. That is precisely why it can be touched. When a crowd worships something, it stops examining it."

The older banker shook his head. "You're betting against the empire."

Fordyce shrugged. "I'm betting against a price," he said. "The empire will survive. The price will not."

He looked at AJ again, and the warmth in his eyes was almost convincing.

"You see, Mr. Sen," Fordyce said, "history is written by those who understand when the room is lying."

AJ said nothing. He didn't trust his voice.

Fordyce turned to the shadowed man near the window.

"Balfour," Fordyce said, "tell our young clerk why we invited him."

The shadowed man—Balfour—shifted slightly. His face was thin, his eyes alert. He looked like a man who could tell you your weakness without raising his voice.

"We invited him," Balfour said, "because numbers are obedient, but men are not. And soon we'll need numbers that can be made to obey."

AJ's blood chilled.

Fordyce waved a hand. "Don't frighten him with poetry," he said lightly. Then, to AJ: "We are planning. And planning creates… correspondence."

He nodded toward the portfolio Lark carried.

"Mr. Sen," Fordyce said, "you will help us draft and copy a series of communications. Discreet ones."

AJ stared. "Sir, I—what kind of communications?"

Fordyce's smile held.

"The kind that reassure," he said. "The kind that persuade. The kind that keep the machine running."

The older banker's fingers drummed on the table. "We shouldn't even be discussing—"

Fordyce cut him off gently. "Everything is discussion," he said. "And discussion is power."

He sat, finally, and the room leaned in as if he had lowered a hook into them.

"Let's speak plainly," Fordyce said. "The market is due for a correction. Not collapse—correction. A fall that will teach humility."

AJ's eyes flicked to the others. Some looked excited. Some looked sick.

"And we," Fordyce continued, "will be positioned on the correct side of that fall."

He lifted his glass again.

"But to stand on that side," he said, "we require credit. We require liquidity. We require the city to remain calm while we move our pieces."

AJ felt the word *pieces* land like a coin in a coffin.

Fordyce looked at him with sudden, almost sincere interest.

"Mr. Sen," Fordyce said, "do you know what a bank run is?"

AJ's mouth went dry. "Yes, sir. When depositors—"

"When depositors panic," Fordyce finished. "When fear travels faster than reason. When the crowd demands metal, not paper."

He leaned forward. "And do you know what causes it?"

AJ hesitated. "Loss of confidence."

Fordyce smiled. "Exactly."

He sat back, satisfied.

"Confidence," Fordyce murmured, almost to himself, "is a currency more delicate than gold."

Balfour spoke again. "And more easily manipulated."

The man with rings laughed nervously. "Surely we aren't—"

Fordyce raised a hand, calming the room.

"We are not villains," he said, voice smooth. "We are merely… realists."

He looked at AJ, and for a moment the room fell quiet, as if waiting for AJ to pass some unseen test.

"Tell me," Fordyce said, "what do you think a clerk is?"

AJ blinked. "Sir?"

"A clerk," Fordyce repeated, "in the grand machinery of commerce. What are you?"

AJ thought of Harrington's face. *A tool he approves of.*

He chose his words carefully.

"I record," AJ said. "I copy. I ensure accuracy."

Fordyce nodded. "Yes."

He leaned closer, voice dropping into something intimate and dangerous.

"And because you record," Fordyce said, "you make reality."

AJ's breath caught.

Fordyce's eyes held his.

"If a number is written in a ledger, the world moves around it," Fordyce continued. "Men act as if it is true. Ships change course. Families eat or starve. Wars are funded. Estates fall."

He smiled slightly.

"So," Fordyce said, "do not underestimate your ink."

AJ's fingers curled around his glass until his knuckles whitened.

The older banker cleared his throat. "We should return to practicalities."

Fordyce waved a hand. "Yes. Practicalities."

He nodded to Lark, who opened the portfolio and slid papers onto the table.

Letters. Drafts. Lists of names.

AJ leaned in despite himself. The writing was neat, the tone polite, the purpose hidden beneath careful phrases.

To assure you of our continued solidity…
To inform you that temporary delays are a matter of routine…
To express our commitment to your long-standing confidence…

Harrington's voice echoed in AJ's mind: *Rumors are a cheap currency.*

These letters were the opposite: expensive currency.

They were designed to purchase calm.

Fordyce gestured at the stack. "You will copy these," he said to AJ. "In a hand that looks official. In a pace that matches urgency without displaying panic."

AJ stared at the drafts, feeling suddenly as if the room had tilted.

"Sir," AJ said carefully, "may I ask… why not have Harrington's clerks do it?"

Fordyce's smile did not change, but the temperature in it did.

"Harrington's clerks are loyal to Harrington," Fordyce said. "You are loyal to your future."

AJ's mouth went dry.

Fordyce leaned back, relaxed again, as if he'd merely explained something about weather.

"You want to rise, Mr. Sen?" Fordyce asked. "Or do you want to remain at the third desk, copying other people's names until your hands turn to bone?"

AJ's heart thudded.

"I want to rise," AJ said before he could stop himself.

Fordyce laughed softly. "There it is," he said. "Honesty."

Balfour's eyes gleamed. "Ambition is useful."

Fordyce slid a small coin purse across the table toward AJ.

AJ didn't reach for it.

Fordyce's voice softened. "Take it. For the trouble. And for your silence."

AJ's throat tightened. He looked at the purse as if it contained a snake.

He thought of his mother's hands, cracked from work. His father's tired eyes. His own small room above the bakery.

He reached out and took the purse.

It was heavier than he expected.

He felt, in that weight, the first invisible chain settle around his wrist.

"Good," Fordyce said, satisfied. "Now."

He turned to the others, shifting the room back into motion.

"We will move quietly," Fordyce said. "We will speak confidently. We will allow the city to continue drinking."

He smiled.

"And when the hangover comes," he said, "we will be sober."

The aristocratic man lifted his glass. "To sobriety, then."

They drank.

AJ drank too, the warmth spreading through his chest like a lie.

Later, much later, AJ left the Crown & Anchor with the coin purse hidden inside his coat and the drafts folded carefully in his satchel.

The night air outside was sharp, smelling of river and soot.

He walked quickly, head down, as if speed could erase the fact that his life had just been touched by a man like Fordyce.

The streets were busy with late revelers and carriage wheels. Somewhere nearby, a woman laughed too loudly. A drunk man sang an off-key song. London was alive, unconcerned.

AJ reached his boarding house and climbed the stairs quietly.

Inside his room, he lit a candle and laid the drafts on his table.

He read them again.

To assure you of our continued solidity…

He stared at the word: *solidity.*

He thought of the vault.

Not empty—but not enough.

He thought of the cabinet full of bills of exchange, promises stacked like bricks.

He thought of Fordyce's smile as he said: *You make reality.*

AJ opened his ledger-copy book and turned to a blank page.

He began to write the first letter, copying the exact phrasing, matching the angle of the handwriting. The quill moved smoothly, obedient.

Halfway through the first paragraph, his hand paused.

A thought rose in him—not fully formed, but sharp enough to hurt:

If these letters were necessary, it meant something was already wrong.

He set the quill down and listened.

Silence.

Just the faint distant city sounds, and the soft crackle of the candle.

He picked the quill up again.

He finished the letter.

Then the second.

Then the third.

Each one was a small architecture of reassurance, built on the assumption that the recipients would not ask the wrong question.

As he wrote, the candle burned lower, and shadows climbed the walls.

When he finished the last letter, AJ flexed his fingers. They ached.

He tied the letters neatly with twine, sealed them, and set them aside.

Then, for reasons he could not name, he opened the deposit ledger copy he'd brought from the bank—a page he was supposed to transfer tomorrow.

He found the line again.

FORDYCE, ALEXANDER

That mountain of ink.

AJ stared at it until his eyes blurred slightly.

Then he did something he hadn't planned to do.

He pulled a clean sheet of paper toward him and wrote, not a copy, not a draft, but a private note—his own handwriting, rougher, less controlled.

A question.

Just one.

If Mr. Fordyce loses… who pays?

He stared at the sentence as if it had appeared on its own.

Outside, in the street below, a carriage rolled by.

Somewhere far off, a bell rang once—lonely, like a warning.

AJ folded the question and tucked it into the lining of his satchel, behind the official letters.

He blew out the candle.

And in the darkness, he lay awake, hearing Fordyce's voice again, smooth as a blade:

I'm not afraid to short a god.

AJ closed his eyes and tried to imagine what it meant to bet against an empire.

He could not.

Not yet.

But somewhere inside him, something had already begun to understand:

Empires were not destroyed by enemies.

They were undone by their own promises.

CHAPTER 3

THREADNEEDLE STREET SMILES

Morning returned to London the way a debt returns—quietly, inevitably, without apology.

AJ walked to Lombard Street with the letters Fordyce had made him copy tucked inside his satchel like contraband. The coin purse sat deeper, hidden under the lining, heavy enough to remind him with every step that he had been purchased in advance.

The city looked normal.

That was the first cruelty of finance: the disaster never arrives wearing a uniform.

Shopkeepers opened shutters. A boy ran with a basket of rolls. Carriages rolled past in glossy indifference. A woman shook a rug from an upstairs window, dust falling like indifferent snow.

And yet, London's rhythm had changed. Not in volume, but in tempo. A half-step quicker. A half-breath shorter. Men in coats paused at corners longer than they used to, not to admire anything, but to listen.

Rumor had become a second weather.

At the bank, the main hall held its disciplined hush, but AJ could feel the strain beneath it like an over-tightened string. Quills scratched faster. The bell rang more often. Clients arrived earlier and lingered longer.

Harrington appeared at AJ's desk before AJ had even removed his coat.

"You were out late," Harrington said.

AJ's stomach tightened. "Sir?"

Harrington's eyes flicked to AJ's satchel. "You look like a man who's been spoken to by someone who matters."

AJ said nothing.

Harrington studied him for one more beat—long enough for AJ to feel the shape of the question Harrington did not ask—then slid a ledger onto the desk.

"Copy today's deposits," Harrington said. "And keep your ears open. Not for gossip—" he tapped the ledger with one finger, "—for patterns."

"Yes, sir."

Harrington leaned closer, voice lowering so that only AJ could hear.

"And if anyone asks you anything you are not certain of," Harrington said, "your answer is simple."

AJ swallowed. "What answer, sir?"

Harrington's expression was flat as a coin.

"I don't know," he said. "And I will find out."

Then he walked away, coat tails cutting clean lines through the air.

AJ opened the ledger.

Names. Figures. Ordinary transactions.

And then the first small thing that didn't feel ordinary.

A deposit.

Withdrawn.

A deposit.

Withdrawn.

The amounts were not dramatic, but the *sequence* was.

Men who used to keep money in the bank were beginning to pull it out in increments—as if they were testing the ground before stepping.

AJ's quill moved.

Copy.

Copy.

Copy.

And while he copied, the bank performed its public face: calm. Competence. The subtle suggestion that the very walls of the building were an argument against panic.

At the counter, a cashier smiled and said, "Of course, sir," with the careful warmth of a physician speaking to a nervous patient.

Behind the counter, the same cashier's hand shook slightly as he counted.

A messenger entered around eleven, boots damp, cheeks flushed from cold.

He did not go to the public counter.

He went straight toward the back doors.

Harrington intercepted him again, took the sealed note, and broke it open without hesitation.

This time AJ watched Harrington's hands.

They did not tighten.

They did something worse.

They stilled.

Harrington read the note twice, the second time slower, as if the words had grown teeth between readings. He folded it, tucked it inside his coat, and turned, scanning the hall the way a man scans a room for exits.

His eyes landed on AJ.

"Sen."

AJ stood quickly, knocking his chair back a fraction too loudly.

Harrington's gaze flicked to the sound, then back to AJ's face.

"Come," Harrington said.

AJ followed, heart climbing into his throat.

They moved through the corridor of closed doors, past names painted in small lettering. Harrington did not pause. He did not knock. He opened one door and ushered AJ in.

Inside was a smaller room with a desk and two chairs, the air smelling of sealing wax and old tobacco. A single window looked down onto a courtyard where servants carried parcels like the parcels were fragile truths.

Harrington shut the door.

Then, for the first time since AJ had met him, Harrington looked… human.

Not emotional. Not panicked.

But concerned in a way that could not be filed neatly into any ledger column.

Harrington placed the note on the desk and did not show it to AJ.

"You went to the Crown & Anchor," Harrington said.

AJ's mouth went dry. "Sir—"

"Don't insult me," Harrington said calmly. "You were summoned. You went. You returned with a new weight in your coat and a new stiffness in your spine."

AJ's cheeks burned. "I didn't— I mean—"

Harrington held up a hand.

"I'm not asking you to confess," Harrington said. "I'm asking you to understand where you are standing."

AJ swallowed. "I understand I'm a clerk."

Harrington's eyes sharpened.

"No," he said. "You understand you're a clerk. That's different."

He walked to the window, looked out as if searching for patience in the courtyard, then turned back.

"Have you ever watched a man drown?" Harrington asked.

AJ blinked. "No, sir."

"It is not the thrashing you'd expect," Harrington said. "It is quiet at the end. A body chooses stillness when it realizes effort is useless."

AJ's pulse thudded louder.

Harrington tapped the note with one finger.

"Do you know what this says?" Harrington asked.

AJ shook his head.

"It says," Harrington replied, "that one of our counterparties is delaying settlement."

AJ frowned. "Settlement—"

"Money that should arrive today," Harrington said. "Not coins in a vault. Paper commitments between houses. A promise that arrives late is not merely late—" he leaned in, "—it is contagious."

AJ's mouth went dry.

Harrington continued.

"First a delay," he said. "Then another. Then a third. And then suddenly you have a room full of men smiling at one another while their throats are closing."

AJ thought of Fordyce's voice: *Confidence is a currency more delicate than gold.*

Harrington watched him.

"You met him," Harrington said. Not a question.

AJ's silence was answer enough.

Harrington sighed, the sound barely more than air.

"Fordyce is a brilliant man," Harrington said. "And brilliance is the most expensive kind of fire."

AJ whispered, "Is it… about the East India Company?"

Harrington's eyes flicked, sharp as a blade.

"Who told you that?" Harrington asked.

AJ hesitated. "He… he spoke of it."

Harrington's face did not change, but AJ saw something shift behind it—a mental calculation.

"Listen to me," Harrington said, voice low. "There are two kinds of knowledge in this city. The kind that makes you rich, and the kind that gets you killed."

AJ's throat tightened. "Which kind is this?"

Harrington held AJ's gaze.

"That depends," Harrington said, "on who you repeat it to."

A knock sounded at the door.

Harrington's posture snapped back into its public shape. He opened the door.

A junior clerk stood there, pale. "Sir—there's a lady at the counter. She—she insists."

Harrington's jaw tightened. "Name?"

The clerk swallowed. "Ashdown, sir. Miss Ashdown."

Harrington's eyes flicked to AJ.

"Come," he said.

They returned to the main hall.

At the public counter stood a woman in a dark coat—not mourning-black, but practical-black. Her hair was pinned cleanly. Her face was composed, but her hands were clenched around a folded paper so tightly the edges had creased.

She did not look like someone who belonged in this hall of male authority.

Which was precisely why she was dangerous to ignore.

Harrington approached with a measured smile.

"Miss Ashdown," Harrington said, voice cordial. "Good morning."

The woman's gaze snapped to him, sharp and steady.

"Mr. Harrington," she said. Her voice was controlled, but it carried—enough that nearby clients began to listen. "I have been here twice this week."

Harrington's smile did not move. "And we are always pleased to see you."

She held out the paper.

"You are delaying payment on a bill," she said. "A bill due yesterday."

Harrington took the paper, glanced at it, and nodded as if it were ordinary.

"This is an invoice tied to West Indies shipment," Harrington said. "There are sometimes—"

"—delays," she cut in, finishing his sentence with a knife of politeness. "Yes. That's what your man said yesterday. And the day before."

Harrington's eyes softened by a fraction. "Miss Ashdown, I assure you—"

"You assure me," she repeated. "But the men who delivered the sugar assure me too. And my warehouse assures me. And my creditors assure me."

Her voice dipped lower, but it sharpened.

"My father is ill," she said. "He cannot stand at this counter and play your… rituals. So I stand here instead."

A murmur moved through the hall like a draft.

Harrington's smile remained.

"Let us speak privately," he said.

"No," she said, and the single syllable landed with weight.

Harrington's eyes tightened.

Miss Ashdown—Eleanor—turned her gaze slightly, letting it touch the listening faces.

"If there is a reason this bill is not being paid," she said, "I would like it stated plainly. Here."

A dangerous moment.

AJ felt it in his bones: the room balancing on the edge of a word.

Harrington did not look at AJ, but his voice shifted—subtle, a signal.

"Sen," Harrington said, "bring the Ashdown account file. Now."

AJ's fingers moved before his mind did. He stood, went to the cabinet, found the Ashdown folder—his hands sure because clerks learned to be sure even when their hearts were not.

He returned and placed the file on the counter.

Eleanor's eyes flicked to him.

For a second she assessed him—quickly, efficiently, the way she had assessed Harrington.

AJ felt exposed.

Harrington opened the file and scanned.

His face remained a banker's face, but AJ saw the tiny tightening at the corner of his mouth.

There was something here.

Harrington looked up.

"Miss Ashdown," Harrington said, voice smooth, "the delay is a matter of routing. The funds are in motion."

Eleanor's gaze did not blink.

"In motion," she repeated. "Like a ship that never arrives."

Harrington's smile thinned.

"We will have it resolved," he said.

"When?" Eleanor asked.

Harrington paused—a fraction too long.

Eleanor saw it.

The pause is where fear breeds.

AJ watched her take in that pause, store it, and convert it into certainty.

Eleanor leaned slightly forward. "Mr. Harrington," she said, voice quiet now, "are your houses… strained?"

The word hit the room like a dropped plate.

Strained.

It was not an accusation.

It was worse.

It was a question that could turn into a stampede.

Harrington's eyes sharpened.

"Miss Ashdown," he said, "our house is sound."

Eleanor did not move.

"Then pay the bill," she said simply.

Harrington's gaze flicked to AJ.

A silent instruction.

AJ's heart hammered. He understood without being told:

If the bank refused here, in public, the rumor would become truth.

Harrington turned to the cashier. "Prepare payment for the Ashdown bill," he said.

The cashier hesitated—one heartbeat too long—then nodded and moved.

Eleanor watched, not satisfied, but alert, like a person watching a physician prepare medicine to be certain it isn't poison.

As the cashier counted and wrote, Eleanor's gaze drifted—briefly, almost accidentally—to AJ's hands.

AJ realized, with a cold clarity, that she was studying him.

Not his face.

His hands.

Ink-stained hands.

Hands that touched the machinery.

Eleanor received the payment with a nod that was not gratitude but acknowledgment.

"Thank you," she said, and the words were formal enough to be harmless.

Then she turned to leave.

At the last second, she glanced back.

Her eyes met AJ's.

Not pleading.

Not accusing.

Just… measuring.

As if she knew the bank's truth lived not in Harrington's smile, but in the clerk who copied numbers all day.

Then she was gone.

Harrington exhaled slowly.

He turned back toward the hall, and the warmth returned to his voice as if he had put a mask back on.

"Gentlemen," he said to the waiting clients, "thank you for your patience."

Patience. The word people used when they meant *fear with manners.*

The hall resumed its quiet movement.

But AJ could feel something had cracked.

A woman had said the dangerous word out loud.

Strained.

And the bank had flinched.

That afternoon, Harrington sent AJ with a sealed packet to Threadneedle Street.

The Bank of England was not far, but it might as well have been another world.

Lombard Street was commerce—loud confidence, constant motion.

Threadneedle Street was authority—quiet, stone, the kind of quiet that implied permanence.

AJ arrived at a building that did not need gold letters to prove it mattered. Its walls were argument enough.

Inside, men moved slower, speaking less. The air felt colder, and not because of the weather.

A clerk at the reception counter examined Harrington's seal and nodded AJ through.

AJ waited in a corridor where the silence had weight.

A door opened. A man in a plain coat stepped out. His face was calm in a way that made AJ uneasy, as though calm here was not a mood but a policy.

"You are from Neal, James, Fordyce & Down," the man said.

"Yes, sir," AJ replied, offering the packet.

The man took it, broke the seal, read quickly.

His face did not change.

He looked at AJ.

"Tell Mr. Harrington," the man said, "that the Bank of England smiles on stability."

AJ swallowed. "Sir?"

The man's eyes were mild.

"A smile," he continued, "is not the same as an embrace."

AJ's throat tightened.

"What does that mean?" AJ asked before he could stop himself.

The man's smile was small and careful.

"It means," he said, "that we observe."

He folded the paper, tucked it away.

"And observation," he added, "is a form of power."

AJ stood very still, feeling as if he had just seen the outline of a larger machine.

He bowed. "Yes, sir."

As AJ turned to leave, he caught a glimpse through an open doorway: a large table, men seated around it, papers spread like maps of invisible war. One of them laughed softly—an elegant laugh, controlled, as if even amusement was managed.

Threadneedle Street smiles on stability.

But it does not bleed for it.

AJ stepped back into the street, the winter air biting his face.

He walked back toward Lombard Street with the strange sensation that the city was being watched from above.

By institutions.

By men.

By something that did not panic because it had the power to decide who would be allowed to survive.

Near evening, AJ returned to his desk and found a new ledger placed there.

No instruction. No note. Just the book.

He opened it.

It was not deposits.

It was something else.

A book of exposures.

A list of counterparties, bills outstanding, obligations piled like snow.

AJ's eyes moved down the page.

He saw names of houses, amounts owed, dates due.

The figures were vast.

And then, halfway down, he saw something that made his stomach fall.

A column labeled **"Expected Inflows"**—money the bank was counting on receiving soon.

And beside it, in thin penciled marks, a series of small changes.

Not ink.

Pencil.

Edited numbers.

Adjusted dates.

A due date moved two days forward.

A large inflow written as if it were certain—when AJ could see, faint beneath the pencil, the original mark: **"uncertain"**.

AJ's breath caught.

This wasn't a mistake.

It was a decision.

A deliberate smoothing of reality.

A lie written gently, so that it looked like housekeeping.

AJ's fingers tightened on the ledger.

He glanced around.

No one seemed to notice him.

No one was meant to.

He looked up toward the partner doors.

Closed.

Behind them, decisions were made.

Outside them, clerks carried those decisions into the world with ink.

AJ thought of Fordyce's words: *Because you record, you make reality.*

And suddenly he understood what Balfour had meant at the Crown & Anchor.

Numbers are obedient, but men are not.

Soon we'll need numbers that can be made to obey.

AJ swallowed hard.

He took a clean sheet of paper and began copying—because that was his job.

But now, every stroke of ink felt like it had a shadow.

And somewhere beyond the bank walls, people like Eleanor Ashdown were beginning to ask the wrong questions out loud.

Strained.

The word was loose in the city now.

And once a word like that escaped, it did not return politely to its cage.

CHAPTER 4

8TH JUNE

On the morning of **8 June**, London woke with a clean sky and a dirty mood.

The kind of day that looks innocent enough to betray you.

AJ arrived early. The bank's doors were still shut, but men were already waiting outside—too many for that hour, clustered in small knots, speaking in quiet bursts. Their faces were not wild. That was what made it worse.

Panic does not always arrive screaming.

Sometimes it arrives wearing a respectable coat and holding a folded newspaper.

AJ pushed past them and entered the bank as the doors opened. The main hall was lit, staffed, arranged. The counters gleamed. The quills were laid out like weapons on an altar.

But the silence had changed.

It wasn't discipline anymore.

It was **listening**.

Harrington stood near the central counter, spine straight, eyes sweeping the room as if searching for fractures in the air. When he saw AJ, he didn't call him over. He didn't need to.

Harrington gave him a look that was instruction without language:

Keep your hands steady. Keep your face blank. If you feel fear, hide it.

AJ took his seat at the third row. He opened his ledger. He dipped the quill.

A bell rang once.

Then again.

Then twice in quick succession.

The front doors swung open and the first rush of clients entered like water finding a crack in a dam.

Not all at once. Not yet.

But enough.

Men approached the counters with polite urgency, each one insisting on coin, each one saying the same thing with different words:

"Just to be safe."

"Only a precaution."

"A temporary matter."

"I'd sleep better."

The cashier smiled and nodded, writing receipts with a hand that looked calm and felt like it belonged to someone else.

AJ watched the lines form and reform, the flow increasing.

A banker's day was normally a machine: deposits, drafts, letters, payment orders.

Today the machine had one purpose:

convert paper into metal.

And metal was finite.

A messenger entered at ten, boots wet, face pale. He moved fast, as if speed could outrun what he carried. Harrington met him before the man reached the partner corridor.

AJ saw the messenger's hand shaking as he presented the sealed letter.

Harrington took it.

Broke it.

Read.

For a moment, Harrington's eyes went somewhere far away—somewhere behind the numbers.

Then he folded the paper, tucked it into his coat, and turned toward the partners' doors.

He knocked once.

A voice inside—muffled.

Harrington entered.

The doors closed behind him.

And the room breathed in, holding itself.

AJ looked down at his ledger and tried to write.

The ink moved, but the numbers refused to remain harmless.

Behind him, a client's voice rose.

Not shouting. Not yet.

But rising.

"I said I want coin," the man insisted. "Not a note. Not a promise. Coin."

A cashier replied, softer. "Sir, we can provide the sum, but it will take—"

"How long?" the man demanded.

A pause.

That was the first true sound of a crisis.

A pause.

AJ's quill hovered. He thought of Eleanor Ashdown, the way she had used a pause like a blade.

The pause is where fear breeds.

Another bell rang. The sound was thin and helpless against the growing murmur.

Then the partner doors opened.

Harrington stepped out.

Behind him, one of the junior partners appeared—Mr. Down, a man who normally wore charm like a well-cut coat. Today his charm looked too small for his body.

Down scanned the hall and lifted his chin slightly, as if reminding the room of who he was.

The reminder did not work.

Harrington moved briskly down the central aisle toward AJ's desk.

"Sen," Harrington said quietly. "Stand. Now."

AJ stood.

Harrington didn't look at the ledger. He looked at AJ's face.

"You wrote letters," Harrington said.

AJ's throat tightened. "Yes, sir."

"To whom?"

AJ's mind raced. "To—clients. Counterparties."

Harrington's eyes narrowed. "Do not lie."

AJ swallowed. "I… copied drafts. At Mr. Fordyce's request."

The name landed between them like a stone thrown into still water.

Harrington's nostrils flared slightly.

Down's voice carried from the counter—too loud for the moment, too cheerful.

"Gentlemen, we assure you there is no cause for—"

The crowd did not respond with calm.

They responded with movement.

A tightening of bodies, a closing of distance.

A man stepped forward.

Then another.

The line shifted from order to **pressure**.

Harrington leaned closer to AJ. His voice was almost gentle.

"Where is Fordyce?" Harrington asked.

AJ blinked. "Sir?"

Harrington repeated it, slower. "Where is Mr. Fordyce."

AJ felt suddenly as if the building had tilted.

"I… I don't know," AJ said, and for once it was the truth.

Harrington's gaze didn't leave him.

"You saw him," Harrington murmured. "You heard him. You were summoned. You were… used." His voice tightened. "And you don't know where he is."

AJ's mouth went dry. "No, sir."

Harrington's eyes flicked past AJ, toward the partner corridor, toward the door that led to the back stairs.

A decision formed inside Harrington like a hardening.

He straightened.

"Stay here," he said to AJ. "Do not move."

Then Harrington turned sharply and strode toward the partner corridor.

The crisis did not wait politely for him to return.

A shout cut through the hall.

"Fordyce is ruined!"

The words came from the back, near the door—someone who had arrived with news, breathless, carrying gossip like a torch.

The room snapped toward the sound.

Down turned. "Who said that?"

Another voice—female, sharp, terrified.

"He's fled! He's fled London!"

That word—**fled**—did what fire does.

It found the driest wood.

The murmurs became a roar.

Men surged toward the counters in a wave of wool and anger. A clerk stumbled, caught, regained his feet only to be pressed back again.

Down's face drained of color.

"Gentlemen!" Down shouted. "Gentlemen—please—"

A fist slammed on the counter.

"Give me my money!"

Another slam.

"Now!"

AJ stood frozen at his desk, watching the room turn from institution to animal.

And then, as if the building itself had decided to confess, a man near the door raised a folded sheet of paper above his head.

A printed notice. Fresh ink. The kind of notice that was never printed unless someone was already bleeding.

He shouted the words as if reading scripture:

"NEAL, JAMES, FORDYCE & DOWN—SUSPENDS PAYMENT!"

For a heartbeat, silence.

Not peace.

Shock.

Then the dam broke.

The roar became a **stampede of voices**, every man suddenly certain he was last, every man suddenly convinced that calm was a luxury he could not afford.

Bodies crushed forward.

A widow screamed.

A clerk cried out as his hand was caught between bodies and counter wood.

Somewhere a glass shattered.

Down's hands trembled as he tried to maintain dignity while losing control of physics.

AJ's chest tightened. He couldn't breathe properly.

Not from fear alone—from the realization that *this* was how paper died.

Not with a grand collapse.

With men shouting for metal.

A cashier tried to close the grille.

The crowd shoved it open.

A man reached through.

The cashier recoiled.

"Stop!" Down shouted. "Stop this at once!"

His voice did nothing.

Power was not in his throat anymore.

Power was in the crowd.

AJ's mind flashed to the vault. The finite stacks. The contained treasure.

Not enough.

He heard Harrington's earlier words, like prophecy:

A promise that arrives late is contagious.

Now promises weren't late.

They were being rejected.

A clerk ran past AJ, face white. "They're emptying the till—" he gasped.

AJ turned instinctively toward the back corridor, where Harrington had gone.

The partner doors were closed.

Then one opened violently.

Harrington emerged.

His face was no longer merely concerned.

It was carved.

He looked older by a decade.

He raised his voice—not shouting, but projecting with a force that snapped heads toward him.

"GENTLEMEN!" Harrington called.

The word "gentlemen" hit the room like a reminder of identity.

For a second, it slowed them.

Harrington moved forward with quick authority. "This house will honor its obligations," he said, voice like steel. "But you must allow order."

A man spat. "Order? We're ruined!"

Another shouted, "Where's Fordyce?"

At that, Harrington's gaze flicked—too briefly—toward AJ.

And AJ understood what that flick meant.

Harrington had searched.

Harrington had learned.

Harrington had found nothing.

Or worse.

Harrington lifted his hands. "Mr. Fordyce is—"

A voice cut in from the doorway—hoarse, ecstatic with fear:

"He's gone to France! He took everything!"

Down's mouth opened, but no sound came out.

Harrington's jaw clenched.

The crowd surged again.

And then, like a disease moving through blood, the bank's internal fear became visible.

A junior clerk dropped a stack of bills. Papers fluttered like wounded birds. The sound of them hitting the floor seemed to confirm what every client already suspected:

The institution was losing its grip.

Eleanor Ashdown appeared at the edge of the hall, pushing in through the crush with a determination that looked insane in the moment and heroic in hindsight. Her face was pale, eyes fixed.

AJ saw her before she saw him.

For a second, their eyes met.

Eleanor's gaze was not accusing.

It was *recognizing.*

So she had been right. She had asked the wrong question and the world had answered.

Harrington moved toward the counter again, trying to keep a line from becoming a mob, trying to keep words from becoming weapons.

Down stumbled back, his hands shaking openly now.

And in that moment, AJ realized something terrifying:

It wasn't that the bank had become weak.

It was that the bank had become **human**.

Human institutions die the way humans die—when everyone sees the fear in their eyes.

AJ's satchel was on the desk. Inside it, his private note—his forbidden question.

If Mr. Fordyce loses… who pays?

AJ didn't need the answer anymore.

He could see it.

The widows. The merchants. The clerks. The people outside this hall who would never know Fordyce's name but would feel his absence like hunger.

The crowd's roar grew louder.

A man climbed onto the bench near the counter, face red, eyes wide.

"They've lied!" he shouted. "They've been lying!"

And people love nothing more than a lie they can finally punish.

Harrington snapped his gaze to AJ again.

This time it was not a flick.

It was a command.

"Sen!" Harrington shouted. "To the back—now—bring the exposure ledger!"

AJ hesitated.

The exposure ledger.

The one with the penciled adjustments.

The deliberate distortions.

If AJ brought it, he became part of whatever would happen next—part of the effort to patch reality back together with more paper.

If he refused, he was refusing in the middle of a storm.

His legs moved anyway.

Obedience was older than courage in his body.

He grabbed the ledger, held it to his chest, and pushed into the corridor toward the back.

As he ran, he heard the front doors shake—hit by hands, hit by bodies.

He heard a shout from outside:

"PAY US!"

The words followed him down the corridor like a curse.

AJ reached the partner room. Inside, two partners stood over the desk, faces gray. Harrington entered behind AJ, slammed the door, and took the ledger from AJ's arms.

He flipped it open like a man looking for a wound.

His eyes scanned the penciled marks.

His face tightened.

One partner whispered, "We need the Bank of England."

The other hissed, "They won't— not for us— not if—"

Harrington turned sharply.

He looked at AJ.

And for the first time, Harrington spoke to him not as a superior to a clerk, but as one human being to another trapped inside the same burning building.

"Mr. Sen," Harrington said quietly, "tell me what Fordyce asked you to copy."

AJ's throat tightened. "Letters," he whispered. "Reassurances. To clients."

Harrington's eyes closed briefly, as if in pain.

"Where are they?" Harrington asked.

"In my satchel," AJ said. "At my desk."

Harrington nodded once, as if that confirmed something he had feared.

"Go," Harrington said. "Get them. And then—" Harrington's voice lowered further, "—do not let anyone see you carry them."

AJ stared. "Sir… why?"

Harrington's gaze was iron.

"Because," Harrington said, "those letters will look like intent."

AJ's chest tightened.

Intent.

Not error.

Not misfortune.

Crime.

The word sat in AJ's mind like a blade pressed gently against skin.

Outside the room, the roar continued. The building shook.

The partners spoke in clipped bursts—liquidity, settlement, collateral, calls—but the words sounded like prayers said too late.

AJ moved to the door.

Then he stopped.

A realization rose in him like bile:

If Fordyce had fled—

If he truly had fled—

Then the letters weren't the only thing that would look like intent.

The penciled adjustments in the exposure ledger—

Those weren't housekeeping anymore.

They were evidence.

AJ looked back at Harrington.

"Sir," AJ said, voice thin, "is Mr. Fordyce… truly gone?"

Harrington did not answer immediately.

That was enough.

Harrington's eyes met his.

And in that look, AJ saw the shape of the truth:

Fordyce hadn't merely lost a bet.

He had **chosen his exit**.

He had written the last line of his own scene and walked offstage.

Leaving everyone else to improvise the fire.

Harrington spoke at last, and his voice was quiet in a way that felt like a funeral.

"Go," Harrington said again. "Before the crowd turns into something we can't name."

AJ opened the door.

The hallway beyond was filled with noise and footsteps and the smell of sweat.

As he ran back toward the main hall, clutching the idea of his satchel like a lifeline, AJ felt something change inside him.

A thin membrane of innocence tore.

He understood now: the world did not run on gold.

It ran on **belief**.

And belief could be stolen—without a pistol, without a sword—

with nothing but a man's smile and a well-timed disappearance.

AJ reached the hall.

It was worse.

The crowd had doubled.

Men pressed against counters like drowning men against a plank.

Someone had overturned a chair. Another man had climbed on the counter itself, shouting as if he could force coin out of wood.

And at the edge of the crush, Eleanor Ashdown stood again, eyes wide, face drained of color, clutching her papers like they were the last proof she existed.

She saw AJ moving.

She saw the satchel strap across his chest.

And in a moment that lasted less than a heartbeat, Eleanor's gaze said something that terrified AJ more than the roaring crowd:

You know.

AJ forced his way to his desk.

His satchel was still there.

He grabbed it.

And as his fingers closed around it, the coin purse inside shifted—heavy, accusing.

Payment for silence.

Payment for complicity.

AJ turned.

The crowd surged.

A man's elbow slammed into his shoulder.

He staggered, clutched the satchel tighter.

As he pushed toward the corridor again, Eleanor moved—fast, decisive—stepping into his path.

"Mr. Sen!" she shouted, her voice barely audible over the roar.

AJ froze.

Eleanor leaned close enough that her words could reach him without becoming public.

"Is it true?" she demanded, eyes burning. "Is he gone?"

AJ's mouth opened.

A hundred answers fought in his throat.

Truth was dangerous.

Silence was easier.

But silence was also a choice.

AJ heard Fordyce's voice in his head, smooth and intimate:

Because you record, you make reality.

Eleanor stared at him, waiting for the world to decide which way it would fall.

AJ swallowed.

Then he said, barely louder than breath:

“I don’t know,” he lied.

Eleanor’s eyes narrowed, not fooled—just forced, by survival, to accept the lie for now.

She stepped back.

AJ pushed past.

As he disappeared into the corridor, he felt the lie settle in his chest like a stone.

Behind him, the bank continued to collapse into noise.

And somewhere in that noise, the world began to understand the oldest truth of credit:

When a promise dies, it does not die alone.

It takes a city with it.

CHAPTER 5

BLACK MONDAY

London did not remember days by their dates.

It remembered them by their **sounds**.

The sound of a bell rung too often.
The sound of iron grilles slamming shut.
The sound of a crowd discovering it has teeth.

The morning after **8 June** arrived like a consequence.

AJ did not sleep. He lay in darkness above the bakery, listening to the city's distant life—carriage wheels, drunken laughter, a dog barking—until each sound felt like a lie London was telling itself: *Everything is normal. Everything is fine.*

At dawn, he rose, dressed, and went back to Lombard Street with the same cold weight in his stomach.

The bank doors were already surrounded.

Not just clients now.

Observers.

Men who had no accounts here but wanted to witness the end of a house. Boys perched on barrels. Shopkeepers pretending to sweep while watching. A pamphleteer with fresh ink on his fingers, eager for a catastrophe he could sell by noon.

London loved a spectacle as much as it loved a profit.

When the doors opened, the crowd surged inside as if the building were a ship and the river had risen.

AJ slipped through the side entrance with the clerks, head down, shoulders tight. He could feel eyes on him—on all of them—like stones thrown silently.

Inside, the main hall was already losing its shape.

Order still existed, but it was **thin** now, stretched like cloth over a frame that had begun to splinter. The counters were crowded. The air was sour with sweat. The polite tone was gone from most voices.

“Coin.”

“Now.”

“No, not a note.”

“I’ve been here since dawn.”

A man shouted at a cashier, his face flushed with humiliation. “Do you think I’m a beggar?”

The cashier’s lips moved, speaking words AJ couldn’t hear, the kind of words that might calm a child or a dying man.

On the far side of the hall, Harrington stood with two other senior clerks, directing like a commander in a siege. His face was calm, but his eyes were too awake.

AJ reached his desk.

His chair had been knocked askew. Ink had spilled, staining the wood like a bruise.

He set his satchel down.

He did not open it.

He couldn’t bear the coin purse’s silent accusation today.

Harrington appeared at AJ’s side.

“You’re here,” Harrington said.

AJ nodded.

Harrington’s voice lowered. “Good. We’ll need your hands.”

“For what?” AJ asked.

Harrington glanced toward the partner corridor. The doors remained shut.

"To write," Harrington said. "To copy. To keep the machine appearing alive."

AJ's throat tightened. "Sir… is it alive?"

Harrington's eyes flicked to him, sharp. "If you ask that question aloud," he said quietly, "you will kill it yourself."

He moved away.

AJ dipped his quill, forced his fingers to work.

But it was hard to pretend to write the future when the present was tearing itself apart.

By midmorning, the first visible wound opened.

A cashier called out quietly: "Mr. Harrington."

Harrington crossed to him.

AJ watched Harrington lean in, listen.

Then Harrington's face did something it almost never did.

It **tightened**.

He straightened and signaled two clerks.

"Close the side till," Harrington said. "Now."

The clerk hesitated. "Sir—"

"Now," Harrington repeated, and his voice was not loud, but it carried.

The clerk moved.

Clients saw.

They always saw.

A murmur traveled like fire through dry grass:

"They're closing."

"They're running out."

"They're—"

The crowd pressed closer.

A man at the counter shouted, "What is this? What are you doing?"

Down emerged from the partner corridor, face pale, collar slightly undone—an intimate sign of a man in trouble.

"Gentlemen," Down said loudly, "please—please remain calm."

A laugh—ugly, sharp—came from somewhere near the door.

"Calm?" someone shouted. "You mean quiet while you steal from us!"

Down's mouth opened.

No words came out that could compete with fear.

The crowd surged again.

A hand reached through the grille and grabbed at a stack of notes.

The cashier yanked them back, face white.

Down stepped forward, and in his panic he did the worst possible thing.

He raised his voice.

"THIS HOUSE WILL HONOR ITS OBLIGATIONS," he shouted.

It sounded like a man insisting he was not dying.

The words did not reassure.

They confirmed.

At the edge of the crowd, Eleanor Ashdown stood again.

AJ spotted her instantly, because she moved differently than the men around her: less noise, more intention. Her coat was the same practical black, but her face looked tighter today, as if she had not slept either.

Her eyes cut through the room.

She was counting.

Not money.

Exits.

People.

The shape of the panic.

When her gaze fell on AJ, she did not shout his name this time.

She simply moved closer, the way a blade moves through cloth.

AJ's throat tightened.

He wanted to avoid her.

He couldn't.

Eleanor reached the edge of his desk, close enough that her voice could slip into his ear.

"You lied," she said, not angry—certain.

AJ's fingers froze over the ledger.

"Miss Ashdown—" he began.

"Don't," she hissed softly. "Don't do the ritual with me."

Her eyes flicked to the partner doors. "Is he gone?"

AJ's mouth went dry.

"I—" he started.

Eleanor leaned closer. "My creditors don't accept 'I don't know,' Mr. Sen," she said. "They accept coin or blood."

AJ swallowed hard. "I truly don't know where he is."

Eleanor studied his face for a heartbeat, then shifted her question—smart, ruthless.

"Do you know whether this house will pay tomorrow?"

AJ felt his stomach drop.

There it was.

The real question.

Not "where is Fordyce," but **how much time is left**.

He looked at the ledger in front of him—numbers, depositors, a story being forced to continue.

He thought of the exposure book with pencil marks.

He thought of Threadneedle Street's mild smile.

A smile is not an embrace.

AJ did the only thing a frightened young man inside a collapsing institution could do.

He told a half-truth.

He lowered his voice.

"Today," AJ whispered, "they are paying."

Eleanor's eyes narrowed. "And tomorrow?"

AJ didn't answer.

Silence is an answer.

Eleanor's jaw tightened.

She straightened, and for a moment she looked older than she had yesterday.

"Thank you," she said, and it wasn't gratitude. It was the tone one uses when receiving a death sentence politely.

She turned and began pushing back toward the crowd.

AJ watched her go, guilt rising in his throat like bile.

She was not here to witness now.

She was here to **act**.

At noon, the bank stopped pretending.

It began with a small announcement, delivered like a prayer:

"Gentlemen," a clerk called from behind the counter, voice strained, "we request your patience while we prepare—"

A man shouted, "Prepare what? More lies?"

The crowd surged.

Someone shoved a stool aside.

A cashier's pen snapped under pressure, the sound tiny and terrible.

Then Harrington climbed onto a chair near the center of the hall.

He did not shout. He did not beg.

He spoke with a calm that was not warmth but **discipline**—the kind of discipline you use when you've accepted you may not be listened to.

"Gentlemen," Harrington said. "This house will suspend payments temporarily."

For one heartbeat, the room froze.

Then the noise arrived like a tidal wave.

"Suspends? What do you mean—"

"That's robbery!"

"My money—"

"My children—"

A man lunged toward the counter.

Another grabbed his coat, pulling him back, and they collided like animals.

A scream rose from the back—high, female.

Then another.

Panic was no longer polite.

It was **physical**.

AJ stood at his desk, quill in hand, watching the hall turn into a storm.

And in the middle of that storm, he saw something that made his blood go cold:

A pair of constables at the doorway.

Not here to protect depositors.

Here to protect the building.

Protect what, AJ thought?

A vault with finite gold?

A cabinet of paper promises?

Or the illusion that London still had control?

Down appeared again near the counter, face wet with sweat.

"We have petitioned for assistance," Down shouted. "We have—"

A man threw something—an apple, perhaps, or a stone. It hit the wood and rolled.

Down flinched, then tried to hold his dignity like a leaking cup.

Harrington's gaze swept the hall and found AJ.

He moved quickly through the chaos, reaching AJ's desk.

"Sen," Harrington said, voice tight, "you're coming with me."

"To where?" AJ asked.

Harrington didn't answer. He grabbed AJ's arm and pulled him toward the back corridor.

AJ stumbled, nearly losing his satchel. He clutched it, the strap biting into his shoulder.

They slipped through the partner doors into the back rooms, where the chaos was muffled but still present—like thunder behind a wall.

In the partner room, the atmosphere was worse than the hall.

Here, no one performed.

Here, men looked like what they were: frightened animals in expensive coats.

One partner paced, hands in hair.

Another sat with his head in his hands, muttering.

Down stood at the desk, arguing with a man AJ hadn't seen before—older, plain coat, calm eyes.

A representative from Threadneedle Street.

The Bank of England.

The calm man looked at Down with mild detachment, as if observing a patient whose fever had become interesting.

Down spoke fast. "We are solvent," he insisted. "We are merely illiquid—temporary, temporary—"

The Threadneedle man raised a hand gently, and the gesture silenced the room more effectively than any shout.

"Mr. Down," the man said softly, "solvency is a story. Liquidity is a fact."

Down's mouth opened. Shut. Open again.

"We require support," Down said, voice cracking. "We require—"

The Threadneedle man's eyes flicked to Harrington.

"And you," he said, "are the clerk who manages the truth?"

Harrington's jaw tightened. "I manage the books, sir."

The Threadneedle man nodded. "Then you understand that faith is not infinite."

Down leaned forward desperately. "Will the Bank assist us?"

The Threadneedle man's expression remained mild.

"We are assisting the market," he said. "Not a single house."

Down's face contorted. "But if we fall—"

"If you fall," the man interrupted gently, "others will learn to stand."

Silence.

That sentence was a blade wrapped in silk.

Harrington's fingers curled into a fist at his side.

The Threadneedle man looked at AJ then, as if noticing him for the first time.

"And you," the man said. "Young clerk."

AJ swallowed. "Yes, sir."

The man's eyes were calm in a way that made AJ feel small.

"Do you know," he asked, "why panic spreads?"

AJ hesitated.

"Because people fear being last," AJ said quietly.

The man smiled faintly. "Exactly."

He turned back to Down.

"We will not ignite the market by rescuing every imprudent man," the man said. "We will provide liquidity where it prevents systemic harm."

Down's voice went hoarse. "What about us?"

The man's mildness hardened into something almost cold.

"Your house," he said, "is not the market."

And in that moment AJ understood the true hierarchy:

Crowds could roar.

Partners could plead.

But institutions like Threadneedle Street could decide which screams mattered.

Harrington grabbed AJ's arm again and pulled him out of the partner room before AJ could process more.

They moved down a narrow corridor to a smaller office where ledgers were stacked like coffins.

Harrington shut the door and turned to AJ.

His face was pale now. Not from panic—Harrington didn't waste emotion that way—but from the weight of inevitability.

"Listen carefully," Harrington said.

AJ nodded.

Harrington's voice lowered. "This house is finished. But the city will not allow the story to end neatly."

AJ's stomach twisted. "What happens?"

Harrington's gaze was fixed, hard.

"There will be inquiries," Harrington said. "There will be accusations. There will be men who need a villain."

AJ's mouth went dry.

Harrington leaned in.

"And Fordyce," Harrington said softly, "has already chosen not to be here for that."

AJ's heart pounded.

Harrington continued. "Do you understand what that means for the people who remain?"

AJ swallowed. "We become—"

"The remaining bodies," Harrington finished. "The remaining hands."

He looked at AJ's satchel.

"And you," Harrington said, "have letters in your handwriting that will look like intent."

AJ's throat tightened. "What do I do?"

Harrington's eyes held his.

"You decide," Harrington said, "whether you want to be a man who survives by silence… or a man who survives by truth."

AJ's chest tightened.

Truth could ruin him.

Silence already had.

Harrington's voice softened by a fraction. "If you keep those letters," he said, "you keep their poison."

AJ's fingers trembled. "If I destroy them—"

"You save yourself," Harrington said. "Or you condemn yourself. I don't know. The world is not just."

He stepped back.

"Now," Harrington said, "go. Before the crowd breaks through the doors and drags someone out to make sense of their fear."

AJ stood frozen.

Then he nodded once.

He turned and left the small office, walking down the corridor with his satchel biting into his shoulder, the letters inside like a load of guilt.

Outside, the bank's roar was still rising.

And beyond Lombard Street, the contagion had already begun—other houses, hearing the name Neal, James, Fordyce & Down spoken with the wrong tone, would feel the same question crawl into their own halls:

Will we be next?

AJ stepped out into the city.

The sky was still clean.

The air still smelled like promises.

But London had begun to learn the difference between a story and a fact.

And somewhere far north, in Scotland, a different bank—built on land and pride and paper—was about to inherit London's disease.

CHAPTER 6

HORSEMAN TO EDINBURGH

The news did not travel like a letter.

It travelled like a fever.

It moved through mouths, through newspapers, through the pause in a sentence when a man says, *have you heard?* It rode on carriage wheels and merchant ships and the thin threads of correspondence that stitched Britain together.

And when it reached Scotland, it did not arrive as "information."

It arrived as **threat**.

EDINBURGH — TWO DAYS LATER

The horse came in hard.

Foam clung to its mouth like lace. The rider's boots were caked with mud. He didn't slow properly at the city edge; he couldn't afford to. He drove the animal forward through streets that smelled of hearth smoke and wet stone, past market stalls and church doors and men who watched him with the instinctive understanding that speed always carried bad news.

He reached a building that wore respectability like armor.

DOUGLAS, HERON & COMPANY
Bankers

The sign was modest. The door was clean. The stone façade looked permanent.

Inside, clerks bent over desks, the same hunched devotion AJ had seen in London. Ink, paper, order.

A bell rang once, and the sound felt comforting.

The rider pushed through and thrust a sealed packet at the reception desk.

"For the partners," he said, breathless.

The clerk stared at the seal, eyes narrowing.

"From London," the rider added, as if the words were a weapon and he needed the clerk to see the blade.

The clerk's face changed.

He did not smile.

He did not ask unnecessary questions.

He stood, took the packet as if it were hot, and disappeared down the corridor toward the partners' room.

The rider slumped against the wall, chest heaving. The horse outside stomped, impatient with human disaster.

A minute passed.

Then two.

The ordinary quiet of the bank began to fracture—not loudly, but in the small signs that trained eyes recognized: a clerk pausing mid-sentence, a head lifting too often, a whisper traveling between desks.

The corridor door opened again.

A senior clerk emerged—older, stern, powdered hair, eyes sharp as needles. His name was **Mr. McLaren**, and he had the kind of face that had never forgiven the world for being uncertain.

He looked at the rider. "You came direct?"

"Yes," the rider gasped. "From the City. Lombard Street. It's—" he swallowed hard, "—it's madness down there."

McLaren's expression remained stiff, but his eyes tightened.

"What house?" he asked.

The rider hesitated—only a heartbeat, but it was enough.

McLaren stepped closer. "What house?" he repeated.

The rider whispered it like a prayer that had failed.

"Neal, James, Fordyce & Down."

The name slid into the room and did what names like that do: it bent the air.

McLaren's lips thinned.

He turned sharply toward the corridor.

"Close the doors," he said.

The clerk beside him blinked. "Sir?"

McLaren's voice hardened. "Close them. Now."

The clerk obeyed, moving to the front entrance.

But the riders of rumor were faster than any clerk.

Outside, Edinburgh already murmured.

Men at the coffeehouses were already leaning closer to one another. Papers were already being unfolded with trembling fingers. Somebody had already told somebody else—*Fordyce has fled*—and that somebody had already exaggerated it into a legend.

By the time the bank doors began to close, a man's voice from outside called:

"Are you paying?"

McLaren froze.

A second voice answered, louder: "Is it true? Is London broken?"

A third voice: "I want my notes redeemed. In coin."

The door shut with a dull, final sound.

Inside, clerks stared at one another.

The illusion of permanence had been interrupted.

McLaren turned to the hall.

"Continue your work," he said.

But his voice did not carry the same authority it would have carried yesterday.

Because everyone could hear the truth under the sentence:

Work cannot stop what is coming.

THE PARTNERS' ROOM — AYR BANK

In the partners' chamber, the air was warmer—fireplace, carpet, polished wood. But the warmth did not comfort. It felt like a room designed for confidence, suddenly hosting doubt.

A tall man stood at the desk, one hand resting on a stack of papers as if they were an altar.

Sir Archibald Douglas—landed, proud, dressed with the quiet arrogance of inherited certainty.

Beside him, a younger partner paced, hands clasped behind his back, jaw clenched like a man forcing himself not to scream.

The sealed packet lay open on the table.

Sir Archibald read its contents once more, slowly, as if the words might change if he stared hard enough.

Then he set it down.

"It says," Sir Archibald said, voice controlled, "that London is ill."

The younger partner snapped. "London is dying."

Sir Archibald's gaze flicked to him. "Mind your language."

The younger man—**Mr. Heron**—laughed once, short and bitter.

"Language?" he hissed. "A bank survives by language. It dies when language fails."

Sir Archibald's fingers tightened on the paper.

"What London suffers," he said, "is the fever of speculation. We are not that."

Mr. Heron stopped pacing. "We are exactly that," he said. "We have extended credit into every corner of Scotland as if paper were seed that grows coin."

Sir Archibald's face hardened. "We extended credit because Scotland required it," he said. "Because the landowners required it. Because trade requires it."

Mr. Heron's eyes burned. "Trade requires confidence," he replied. "And confidence is precisely what London has lost."

A third partner—older, heavy-set, face lined with worry—cleared his throat.

"Gentlemen," he said quietly, "we must prepare for redemption requests."

Sir Archibald's jaw tightened. "We have coin," he said.

The older partner swallowed. "Not enough," he whispered.

Silence.

Sir Archibald stared at him as if the man had spoken blasphemy.

"We have land," Sir Archibald said, voice firm now, as if he could argue with reality. "We have estates. We have solid collateral."

Mr. Heron's laugh was sharper.

"Land is not liquidity," he said. "You cannot melt an estate into coin by noon."

Sir Archibald's eyes narrowed. "You speak like a London man."

Mr. Heron stepped forward. "I speak like a man who understands that we built a bank on the assumption that no one would ever ask for coin all at once."

A knock at the door.

McLaren entered without waiting for permission, face pale in a way that made even Sir Archibald stiffen.

"Sir," McLaren said, voice low, "there are men outside."

Sir Archibald's chin lifted. "How many?"

McLaren hesitated. "Dozens. Possibly more. They are asking to redeem."

Sir Archibald's mouth tightened.

"Open the doors," he said.

Mr. Heron snapped his gaze to him. "Are you mad?"

Sir Archibald's eyes flashed. "We do not hide," he said. "This is Scotland."

Mr. Heron's voice was tight. "This is finance."

Sir Archibald ignored him and looked at McLaren.

"Let them in," Sir Archibald said. "We will show them we are sound."

McLaren nodded and left.

Mr. Heron turned to the older partner. "How much coin do we have in the till?"

The older partner's eyes lowered. "Less than the City would demand," he admitted.

Mr. Heron's jaw clenched.

Sir Archibald waved a hand. "We will pay those who come," he said. "Then they will tell the others we pay."

Mr. Heron's face hardened. "Or they will tell the others they must come now," he said. "To be first."

Sir Archibald's voice sharpened. "Enough."

But enough was never enough when fear began to calculate.

THE FRONT HALL — AYR BANK

The doors opened.

Men entered.

Respectable men. Merchants. Farmers. Small landholders. A widow with a scarf pulled tightly around her neck. A priest. They did not look like a mob.

They looked like Scotland.

That was the second cruelty: panic wears the face of your neighbors.

McLaren stood behind the counter, his posture rigid.

"How may we help you?" he asked with forced politeness.

A man stepped forward.

"I want my notes redeemed," he said. "In coin."

McLaren smiled as if it were ordinary. "Of course, sir."

Another man stepped forward immediately.

"So do I," he said.

And another.

"And I."

The line formed fast.

Too fast.

McLaren's fingers moved, counting coin, writing receipts. His smile did not falter, but his eyes did. They began to flick toward the door too often.

Because more people kept coming.

A clerk leaned in and whispered in McLaren's ear.

McLaren's jaw tightened.

He glanced toward the partners' corridor.

Then he returned to counting.

Coin left the bank in small handfuls.

It felt like watching blood drain drop by drop.

Outside, as the first men emerged holding coin, they did not look reassured.

They looked **triumphant**.

And triumph is contagious.

A man outside shouted: "They're paying! Hurry!"

The line doubled.

Inside, the coin stacks shrank.

McLaren's mouth went dry.

A clerk dropped a coin, and the small clink against the floor sounded louder than any bell.

McLaren felt every ear twitch.

Sir Archibald entered the hall, attempting dignity.

"Gentlemen," he said, voice clear, "we assure you—"

A man cut him off, not rude, just urgent.

"Then pay us," he said.

Sir Archibald's jaw tightened.

McLaren leaned slightly toward him, whispering without turning his head.

"Sir," McLaren said, voice tight, "we are draining the till."

Sir Archibald's face stiffened.

Mr. Heron appeared behind him, eyes blazing.

"We must slow it," Mr. Heron hissed. "We must—"

Sir Archibald lifted his chin. "We must not show fear," he said.

Mr. Heron's voice was low, furious. "Fear is already here," he said. "It's standing in line."

BACK TO LONDON — AJ

While Scotland began to tremble, AJ stood in a narrow alley behind Neal, James, Fordyce & Down, holding a bundle of letters like a funeral shroud.

Harrington's words repeated in his mind:

If you keep those letters, you keep their poison.

The alley smelled of damp brick and refuse. A stray cat watched him with indifferent eyes.

AJ's hands shook as he opened the bundle.

The letters were so polite.

So careful.

So deadly.

To assure you of our continued solidity…

He thought of Eleanor Ashdown's face, pale and fierce.

He thought of the widow screaming in the hall.

He thought of Threadneedle Street's mild smile.

A smile is not an embrace.

AJ struck a match.

The flame flared small and fragile.

It looked like nothing.

Like a child's trick.

He touched the flame to the edge of the first letter.

The paper curled.

The ink blackened.

Smoke rose, thin as a confession.

AJ watched the words vanish into ash.

For a moment he felt relief.

Then he felt something worse.

He felt that he had just destroyed the only proof that he had been asked to lie.

He had saved himself.

Or he had removed evidence.

He didn't know which.

As the last letter burned, AJ heard footsteps behind him.

He turned sharply.

A man stood at the alley's mouth.

Not a clerk.

Not a client.

A stranger in a plain coat, eyes calm, face unreadable.

He watched the smoke.

Then he looked at AJ.

"Mr. Sen," the man said softly.

AJ's blood went cold.

"How do you know my name?" AJ asked.

The man's mouth curved slightly, not a smile—an acknowledgment.

"London is small when it is frightened," the man said.

AJ clutched the remaining ash, as if he could hide it.

The man stepped closer.

"I represent interests," he said. "Interests that would like to understand what happened."

AJ's throat tightened. "I'm only a clerk."

The man nodded.

"Clerks," he said, "are where truth goes when it wants to hide."

The words struck AJ like a slap.

The man extended a gloved hand.

"Come," he said. "Someone would like to speak with you."

AJ's mind raced.

If he refused, he might be dragged.

If he went, he might be consumed.

He glanced down at the ash in his palm.

The last of the letters.

The last of the lies.

He closed his fist, crushing the ash into dust.

Then he stepped forward.

Far north, in Scotland, the coin stacks continued shrinking.

And in London, AJ walked toward an unknown meeting, realizing too late that in a credit crisis, there were always men who profited from disaster—

and they always wanted a clerk to hold the pen.

CHAPTER 7

LAND IS NOT LIQUIDITY

Scotland had always believed itself different.

More stubborn. More solid. Less intoxicated by London's glittering games.

But finance does not respect pride.

It respects only one thing:

repayment on demand.

AYR — THE SECOND MORNING

The doors opened again, and the line was already there.

Longer than yesterday.

Quieter than yesterday.

That was how panic matured—less shouting, more certainty. Men did not come to argue now. They came to *extract.*

McLaren stood behind the counter with a tight jaw and tired eyes. He had been awake all night balancing tills, checking reserves, counting coin like a man counting ammunition.

Coin stacks were smaller this morning.

And the crowd was larger.

The first man stepped forward. He didn't even greet.

"Redeem my notes," he said.

McLaren forced a smile. "Of course, sir."

The man didn't smile back. "All of it."

McLaren's fingers moved, but his mind was screaming numbers.

This is not a request, he thought.

This is a leak turning into a rupture.

The next man stepped forward immediately, shoving his notes onto the counter.

"And mine."

Then another.

"And mine."

The line advanced with a rhythm that felt like an executioner's drum.

McLaren paid them.

He had to.

Every refusal was a match tossed onto dry tinder.

But every payment was blood leaving the body.

In the partners' room, Sir Archibald Douglas stood by the window, watching the street as if his gaze could intimidate fear.

Mr. Heron paced like a trapped animal.

The older partner sat at the desk, face gray, hands shaking slightly as he tried to write requests for support.

"London is ill," Sir Archibald repeated, as if repetition could turn denial into shield. "We are not London."

Mr. Heron snapped. "We are worse," he said. "We are London without Threadneedle Street."

Sir Archibald turned sharply. "Mind your tone."

"My tone?" Mr. Heron hissed. "The till is bleeding. That is my tone."

The older partner looked up, voice thin. "We must stop paying in full," he whispered.

Sir Archibald's eyes hardened. "And announce to Scotland that we are afraid?" he said. "Never."

Mr. Heron leaned over the desk. "Then we die," he said.

Sir Archibald's jaw clenched.

He hated the word *die* in a room designed for permanence.

A knock.

McLaren entered, face pale.

"Sir," McLaren said quietly, "we have less than half of yesterday's coin."

Sir Archibald's expression did not change. That was his gift and his curse.

"How long," Sir Archibald asked, "if the line continues at this pace?"

McLaren swallowed. "Hours," he admitted.

The older partner's hand trembled more violently.

Mr. Heron stopped pacing. He stared at Sir Archibald as if daring him to accept reality.

Sir Archibald stared back.

For a moment, two kinds of power faced each other:

Inherited pride.

And arithmetic.

Arithmetic always wins.

Sir Archibald spoke at last, voice measured.

"We will send riders," he said. "To Edinburgh. To Glasgow. To our friends. To the estates."

Mr. Heron's laugh was harsh. "To do what?" he demanded. "Ask landowners to bring coin from their chimneys?"

Sir Archibald's eyes narrowed. "We will call in loans," he said.

Mr. Heron's face twisted. "Call in loans?" he repeated. "In a panic?"

Sir Archibald's voice sharpened. "We require liquidity."

Mr. Heron's voice dropped dangerously. "You will destroy the very people whose confidence you want," he said. "You will force them into collapse to save your own pride."

Sir Archibald stepped forward. "This bank was built to elevate Scotland," he said. "We extended credit to men who had only land. We gave them air to breathe."

Mr. Heron stared. "And now," he said softly, "you are taking their air back."

Sir Archibald's face tightened, but he did not retreat.

"Do what must be done," he said.

McLaren nodded, grim.

The order left the room like a curse.

THE LOAN CALLS

By afternoon, the letters began arriving.

Not polite invitations.

Demands.

Landowners opened them at breakfast tables and felt their stomachs drop.

Merchants read them in warehouses and went cold.

Farmers stared at them in kitchens and realized they were being asked to pay cash they did not have.

Because the bank—once the giver—had become the taker.

The calls were phrased with professional courtesy, but the message underneath was simple:

Pay now, or we will ruin you.

And the men receiving them did what frightened people always do.

They ran to the bank.

Not to repay.

To withdraw what they could before the bank swallowed them whole.

The line grew longer.

The till shrank faster.

Panic fed itself.

THE HALL — THE MOMENT IT TURNS

At the counter, a small landholder named **Gavin Reid** placed his notes down carefully.

He was not wealthy. His hands were calloused. His coat smelled faintly of sheep.

"I'd like them redeemed," he said, voice steady.

McLaren nodded, reached for coin.

His fingers paused.

He looked toward a clerk. The clerk shook his head—tiny, almost invisible.

McLaren's mouth went dry.

He turned back to Gavin Reid.

"Sir," McLaren said carefully, "we can provide a portion today, and the remainder—"

Gavin stared. "A portion?"

McLaren forced his smile. "A temporary arrangement—"

Gavin's eyes sharpened. "No," he said quietly. "No, I want it all."

McLaren's smile flickered.

Behind Gavin, the line listened.

Panic always listens.

McLaren leaned in. "Sir," he whispered, "please—"

Gavin's voice rose—not a shout, but a blade of sound.

"They won't pay," he said, turning slightly so the line could hear. "They won't pay in full."

The hall froze for one heartbeat.

Then the murmur rose like water pouring through a crack.

"They won't?"

"Did you hear?"

"They're refusing—"

McLaren's voice lifted, trying to regain control.

"Gentlemen—gentlemen, please—"

A man near the back laughed, sharp and ugly.

"Gentlemen? We're beggars now!"

The line surged forward.

McLaren stepped back instinctively.

That step was fatal.

Fear saw it.

Fear interpreted it correctly.

Fear became certainty.

Within minutes, the respectable line became a crush of bodies, and the bank hall became what every bank fears becoming:

A place where words no longer matter.

A clerk shouted for the doors to be closed.

Another shouted no—closing doors meant admitting.

Too late.

Someone slammed a fist on the counter, hard enough to rattle the wood.

"PAY US!"

Another fist.

"PAY!"

A woman screamed.

A child cried.

McLaren's hands shook so badly coins slipped and rolled across the floor.

The tiny metallic clinks became a soundtrack of humiliation.

Sir Archibald Douglas entered the hall, jaw set like granite.

He raised his hands. "Scotland!" he shouted. "Scotland does not panic!"

A man shouted back, "Scotland bleeds the same!"

Sir Archibald's face went rigid.

Mr. Heron pushed through behind him, eyes blazing.

"We must suspend," Mr. Heron hissed.

Sir Archibald's voice rose. "Never."

Mr. Heron grabbed his arm. "Then we are dead men," he said through clenched teeth.

Sir Archibald shook him off.

And that—*the partners fighting in public*—was the moment the crowd understood:

The bank was no longer a single body.

It was a corpse arguing with itself.

The crush intensified.

McLaren shouted at clerks. "Bar the doors!"

A clerk hesitated, then moved.

The doors began to close.

A man shoved his shoulder into them.

Another man joined.

The doors slammed shut—not from calm, but from violence.

Outside, fists pounded.

Inside, fear became a physical thing.

And then, finally, Mr. Heron stepped forward, voice booming, desperate, real.

"THE BANK WILL SUSPEND PAYMENTS," he shouted.

For a heartbeat, the hall went silent.

Then the noise returned, louder, uglier—because now the truth had been spoken aloud.

Men began to cry.

Men began to curse.

Men began to understand the word that destroys generations:

ruin.

LONDON — AJ AND THE "INTERESTS"

While Scotland collapsed, AJ walked through London as if he were being guided by invisible hands.

The stranger in the plain coat did not hurry him. He did not threaten him. That made the threat worse—it implied certainty.

They moved through narrow streets, away from Lombard, away from the public spectacle, toward quieter districts where power did not advertise itself with noise.

At last they entered a townhouse whose front door was unremarkable.

Inside, everything was subdued luxury: dark wood, soft carpets, paintings that watched you.

AJ's shoes felt too loud.

The stranger led him into a room where two men sat at a table covered with papers.

One man was thin and elegant, hair powdered, hands clean. The other was broader, face heavy with authority, eyes sharp.

Neither looked surprised to see AJ.

The elegant man spoke first.

"Mr. Sen," he said, voice warm enough to seem kind. "Thank you for coming."

AJ swallowed. "Who are you?"

The broader man answered, voice flat.

"We are men who prefer markets not burn down," he said.

The elegant man smiled faintly. "And we are men who prefer narratives not drift into… chaos."

AJ's stomach tightened. "Narratives?"

The elegant man's gaze softened, almost sympathetic.

"When a house fails," he said, "the city demands a story. If the story is uncontrolled, the story spreads panic."

The broader man leaned forward. "Panic," he said, "destroys good houses with bad ones."

AJ's mouth went dry.

The elegant man gestured at the table.

Letters. Lists. Names. Drafts.

"The crisis is already expanding," the elegant man said. "Houses will fall. Trade will seize. Credit will freeze."

He looked at AJ.

"And someone," he continued, "must be blamed in a manner that limits contagion."

AJ's blood went cold.

"You want a scapegoat," AJ said before he could stop himself.

The elegant man's smile did not change.

"I want a focal point," he corrected. "A story the city can digest."

The broader man's voice was harder.

"Fordyce is gone," he said. "So we require substitutes."

AJ's breath caught.

The elegant man leaned in slightly. "You wrote letters," he said gently.

AJ's throat tightened. "I—copied drafts."

"Drafts that reassure," the elegant man said. "Drafts that could be construed as deception."

AJ felt the room tilt.

He heard Harrington's words again: *Those letters will look like intent.*

AJ's voice came out thin. "I destroyed them."

The elegant man blinked, then smiled as if he'd been given a gift.

"How efficient," he murmured.

The broader man's eyes narrowed. "You destroyed evidence?"

AJ's hands clenched. "I destroyed lies," he said, trying to sound like the kind of man who had principles.

The elegant man nodded thoughtfully. "A noble framing."

He folded his hands. "Mr. Sen," he said, "we are not here to punish you. We are here to offer you safety."

AJ stared. "At what cost?"

The elegant man's smile grew softer.

"You will testify—informally," he said, "to the version of events that reduces systemic fear. You will confirm that the house's failure was the result of one man's imprudence."

AJ's throat tightened. "But it wasn't one man."

The broader man's voice cut in, cold.

"History rarely is," he said. "But history is written as if it is."

AJ felt sweat gather at the base of his spine.

The elegant man's voice became almost kind.

"You are a clerk," he said. "You have no shield except the shield we offer you. Without it, you may find yourself questioned by authorities eager to appease the crowd."

AJ swallowed. He could picture it: dragged out, blamed, crushed.

"And if I refuse?" AJ asked.

The broader man stared. "Then you become… available," he said simply.

Silence.

AJ's heart hammered.

The elegant man continued, gentle as poison.

"Do you understand now why we invited you?" he asked.

AJ's voice was barely audible. "You want my pen."

The elegant man smiled.

"We want your reality," he said.

SCOTLAND — THE AFTERMATH

As Ayr Bank suspended payments, the effect rippled outward like a stone thrown into water.

Landowners who had built their lives on bank credit found their foundations vanish.

Merchants who relied on bills of exchange saw them turn to ash.

Debtors were called.

Creditors demanded.

Families argued at dinner tables with voices that sounded like strangers.

Men who had walked proudly now walked with eyes lowered.

Scotland's confidence—so carefully built—began to crack.

And somewhere in Edinburgh, McLaren sat with his head in his hands, knowing the truth that no sermon could erase:

A bank cannot pay with land.

A bank cannot pay with pride.

A bank can only pay with what is demanded when it is demanded.

Land is not liquidity.

AJ stood in the London townhouse, feeling the invisible machinery close around him.

The elegant man extended a paper across the table.

Not a contract, not an oath—something softer and more dangerous.

A statement.

A version of events.

A story to be signed.

AJ stared at the paper.

He thought of Eleanor Ashdown.

He thought of Gavin Reid, the landholder with sheep-scented hands.

He thought of Harrington's rigid dignity as the city roared.

He thought of the ash in his palm.

And he realized something with sudden clarity:

This crisis was not just destroying banks.

It was **rearranging truth**.

AJ reached for the pen.

His fingers hovered.

And in that hover, he felt the whole world balance on the point of ink.

CHAPTER 8

AMSTERDAM FREEZES

Credit always looks local—until it fails.

Then you discover the world is a single nervous system, and one city's pain becomes another city's paralysis.

LONDON — THE PEN

The statement lay on the table like a quiet weapon.

The elegant man watched AJ as if watching a candle near dry cloth—patient, certain, almost bored by the inevitability.

The broader man did not watch AJ's face.

He watched AJ's hands.

Because hands decide.

AJ read the statement once.

Then again.

It was clean. It was plausible. It was framed like a physician's report: one cause, one patient, one failure.

Alexander Fordyce, imprudent speculator.
A misjudged position.
An unfortunate run.
A temporary strain, now contained.

Contained.

AJ almost laughed.

Contained was what men said when they meant, *Please stop looking.*

The elegant man leaned in, voice gentle.

"You understand," he said, "that clarity calms markets."

AJ kept his eyes on the paper. "This isn't clarity," he said quietly. "It's a story."

The broader man's voice cut in. "A story is what keeps other houses from burning."

AJ looked up. "And who decides which houses deserve not to burn?"

The broader man stared back. "The houses that matter," he said.

Silence.

That sentence explained everything.

AJ's throat tightened. "What about the people?"

The elegant man smiled faintly, almost sad.

"The people," he said, "will suffer regardless. We are attempting to prevent suffering becoming contagious."

AJ stared at the paper again, and in the statement he saw something worse than lies.

He saw **strategy**.

If the crisis had a single villain, then the system could be preserved.

If the system could be preserved, those who sat at tables like this could continue to own tomorrow.

AJ's fingers curled around the pen.

He thought of Eleanor Ashdown's face, the controlled fury.

He thought of Scotland's pride breaking into a stampede.

He thought of the vault's finite gold.

And he understood:

If he refused, he would become a victim.

If he signed, he would become a weapon.

AJ lowered the pen.

The nib touched the paper.

Ink began to move.

The elegant man's eyes softened, satisfied.

AJ signed.

Not boldly.

Not confidently.

Like a man placing his hand on a blade to prevent it from falling elsewhere—knowing it would cut him anyway.

When he finished, he slid the paper back across the table.

The elegant man folded it and tucked it into a portfolio as if it were a mere receipt.

"Wise," he said.

The broader man stood. "Now you will go back," he said. "And you will continue to work."

AJ blinked. "Work? The house is finished."

The broader man's gaze was flat. "The house is finished," he agreed. "But the city is not."

The elegant man leaned in one last time.

"Mr. Sen," he said softly, "do you know what freezes trade?"

AJ swallowed. "Fear."

The elegant man smiled. "Uncertainty," he corrected gently. "Fear is useful. Uncertainty is lethal."

He patted the portfolio. "You have reduced uncertainty."

AJ stood slowly.

His legs felt heavy.

The stranger in the plain coat reappeared at the door, a silent escort.

As AJ was guided back out into London's streets, he realized with a cold clarity that the crisis had begun to do what crises always did:

It was selecting who would be protected, and who would be abandoned.

And it had just selected him—for now.

THE CONTAGION ROUTE

London's failure was not merely a London event.

It was a message written in ink across a network of trade:

Bills of exchange. Correspondence. Trust.

By the time the statement AJ signed began circulating in the right rooms, the damage had already moved beyond England.

Ships had been financed with paper, not coin.

Cargoes had been promised to men who had promised payment to others.

A single delayed settlement in London meant a merchant in Amsterdam might not be paid on time, which meant his creditor might not meet an obligation in Hamburg, which meant a warehouse might close in Rotterdam.

Trade finance is a chain.

And chains snap at their weakest link.

AMSTERDAM — THE ICE

Amsterdam's canals moved slowly.

Too slowly.

The water carried reflections of tall, narrow buildings—merchant houses that had outlived wars, storms, and kings.

These houses had survived by one religion:

reputation.

Inside one of them, a merchant named **Jan van der Velde** stood over a desk, staring at a bill of exchange as if it were a letter announcing a death.

The bill was drawn on a London house.

It was due.

It was not being honored.

Jan's clerk, a young Dutchman with anxious hands, whispered, "They say London houses are failing."

Jan's jaw tightened. "They say many things," he replied.

But he could not ignore the evidence in his own fingers.

Paper that should have been as good as coin now felt like cloth that had been soaked and torn.

A knock at the door.

Jan's wife entered quietly, her face tight. "There is a man downstairs," she said. "From the sugar syndicate."

Jan's stomach sank.

"Send him up," he said.

A moment later, the man arrived—well dressed, but with eyes that had learned to count panic.

"Jan," the man said, forcing cheerfulness. "We've heard—"

"Everyone has heard," Jan cut in.

The man's smile tightened. "We need to discuss your obligations," he said.

Jan stared. "My obligations depend on London," he said. "And London—"

The man raised a hand. "London is London," he said. "Amsterdam is Amsterdam. We pay our obligations here."

Jan felt the ice forming.

This was how finance froze: not with dramatic collapse, but with men refusing to accept that *someone else's problem* could become theirs.

Jan spoke carefully. "The bill will settle," he said. "It is delayed."

The man leaned forward. "Delayed," he repeated. "Do you know what delayed means this week?"

Jan didn't answer.

The man's voice became softer, more dangerous.

"It means," he said, "you become the delay."

Jan swallowed hard.

When the man left, Jan turned to his clerk.

"Cancel new credits," Jan said.

The clerk blinked. "Sir?"

"Cancel them," Jan repeated. "No new extensions. No new acceptances. Demand hard settlement."

The clerk's face drained. "Sir, if we demand—"

"If we do not," Jan said, voice tight, "we drown with them."

The clerk moved.

And so did the city.

Merchant houses began refusing new bills.

Brokers began demanding cash.

The invisible machine of trust slowed, then jammed.

Amsterdam's trade did not collapse with a scream.

It **stiffened**.

Like a body going cold.

LONDON — ELEANOR FEELS IT

Eleanor Ashdown did not need Amsterdam to be named to feel its frost.

She felt it in her warehouse.

In men who suddenly insisted on payment in coin.

In sailors who demanded wages up front.

In a supplier who smiled apologetically while tightening a noose.

She stood in her office above the warehouse, looking at ledgers that no longer balanced because the world had stopped agreeing on the same reality.

Her father coughed in the next room—thin, persistent, like a reminder of mortality.

Eleanor held a letter that had arrived that morning: a polite refusal from a correspondent.

Due to current conditions, we regret we cannot extend further credit at this time…

She crumpled it in her fist, then flattened it again.

Rage was useless.

She needed leverage.

She needed information.

And there was one man in London who sat near the machinery.

A clerk.

Eleanor grabbed her coat and left.

LONDON — AJ RETURNS TO THE RUINS

AJ returned to Lombard Street like a man returning to a burned house to look for something he was too late to save.

The bank building still stood.

It would always stand.

Stone survives.

But inside, the life was gone.

The main hall was quieter now—not calm, but exhausted. The crowds had dispersed into other disasters. The counters were occupied by clerks sorting papers that would become lawsuits. The smell of sweat had been replaced by the smell of ink and defeat.

Harrington stood at a desk near the back, shoulders slightly slumped—his first visible sign of fatigue.

When he saw AJ, he did not greet him with anger.

He greeted him with something closer to relief.

"You're alive," Harrington said.

AJ swallowed. "Yes, sir."

Harrington's eyes narrowed. "Where have you been?"

AJ hesitated.

The truth was dangerous.

So he chose a different truth.

"I was questioned," AJ said quietly.

Harrington's face hardened. "By whom?"

AJ looked at Harrington and realized: if he named the "interests," he might put Harrington in danger too.

"I don't know their names," AJ said. "But they were not police."

Harrington's jaw clenched.

He leaned in, voice low. "Did you give them anything?"

AJ's throat tightened.

He thought of the statement.

He thought of ink becoming reality.

He nodded once.

Harrington's eyes closed briefly.

When he opened them, the anger was there—but beneath it, something else.

Disgust.

Not at AJ.

At the system.

"At least you're honest with me," Harrington said quietly.

AJ's voice came out thin. "What happens now?"

Harrington gestured at the stacks of papers. "Now," he said, "we become fuel for lawyers."

He picked up a ledger and tapped it with a finger.

"And for historians," he added bitterly. "Men who will write this as if it were an accident."

AJ swallowed.

Harrington studied him, then spoke softly.

"You destroyed the letters?" Harrington asked.

AJ nodded.

Harrington's gaze stayed on AJ for a long moment.

"Smart," Harrington said finally. "Or cowardly. It's hard to tell anymore."

AJ flinched.

Harrington's voice softened again. "Either way," he said, "you are now inside the story."

AJ's stomach tightened. "I didn't want to be."

Harrington's smile was bleak. "No one does," he said. "That's why it happens."

THE FIRST TRUE SHIFT

Outside, trade continued to freeze.

Bills went unpaid.

Merchants tightened credit.

Ships waited.

And somewhere, men at tables like the one AJ had sat at began deciding which houses would be allowed to thaw.

AJ had reduced uncertainty for them.

Now, they would use that certainty like a lever.

And when a lever moves, something breaks.

As AJ stood in the wreckage of the bank, Eleanor Ashdown entered the hall.

She did not call his name.

She walked straight toward him with the calm of a woman who had decided that politeness was too expensive.

AJ saw her.

His throat tightened.

Eleanor stopped in front of him, eyes burning.

"You're still here," she said.

AJ didn't know whether it was accusation or surprise.

Eleanor's voice dropped.

"I need to know," she said, "who is controlling this."

AJ swallowed hard.

Harrington watched them from a distance, expression unreadable.

AJ realized: this was the moment the crisis became something else.

Not just bank failure.

Not just panic.

But politics.

Power.

The manipulation of truth.

AJ looked at Eleanor and felt the weight of what he had signed.

He had helped shape the story.

Now Eleanor wanted the real one.

He opened his mouth.

And somewhere, far away, Amsterdam's trade continued to stiffen.

The world on credit was freezing, one refusal at a time.

CHAPTER 9

WHO GETS SAVED?

A crisis does not treat people equally.

It pretends to, at first—like a storm that falls on everyone. But then you watch carefully and you learn the truth:

Storms have patterns.

And so does mercy.

LOMBARD STREET — THE QUESTION

Eleanor Ashdown stood in the ruined hall of Neal, James, Fordyce & Down like she belonged there.

Not because the bank welcomed her—banks welcomed only money and men—but because she refused to be moved by discomfort.

AJ looked at her and felt the cruel geometry of his position:

If he told her too much, he would invite danger.

If he told her too little, he would invite her ruin.

Eleanor didn't give him time to hide behind silence.

"Who controls this?" she asked again, voice quiet but cutting.

Harrington was close enough to hear. He didn't interrupt. He didn't rescue AJ. He just watched, as if waiting to see what kind of man AJ would become.

AJ swallowed. "There are… men," he said carefully. "Men who decide which stories circulate."

Eleanor's eyes sharpened. "Names."

AJ felt sweat gather under his collar.

"I don't know their names," AJ lied.

Eleanor's gaze didn't blink.

"You're a clerk," she said softly. "You know the value of a detail. You know the difference between not knowing and not saying."

AJ's jaw tightened. "If I say it aloud," he whispered, "it becomes a weapon aimed at me."

Eleanor leaned closer. "And if you don't," she whispered back, "the weapon is aimed at everyone else."

AJ looked away for a second, his eyes landing on the counters where desperate hands had pounded for coin.

He could still hear it in memory—*Pay us! Pay us!*—as if the wood retained the bruise.

He looked back at Eleanor.

"The Bank of England is watching," AJ said quietly.

Eleanor's mouth tightened. "I know that," she said. "They always watch."

AJ hesitated, then added, "And there are private men. Merchants. Financiers. They meet in rooms that don't appear on maps."

Eleanor's eyes flicked toward the partner corridor. "And you've been in one of those rooms."

AJ didn't answer.

Eleanor took that as confirmation.

"Then you've met them," she said. "And you've been used."

AJ's throat tightened.

Eleanor's voice softened just enough to feel like a hand offered rather than a blade.

"Mr. Sen," she said, "my father will not survive this winter if our credit freezes. My warehouse will be seized. My workers will starve. My creditors will not accept poetry."

She held AJ's gaze.

"So I am asking you," she said, "not as a woman, not as a merchant—"

She swallowed once.

"As a person," she finished. "Who gets saved?"

The question hit AJ harder than any shout in the hall.

Because it wasn't finance anymore.

It was moral.

AJ's voice came out quiet. "The ones with connections," he admitted. "The ones whose ruin would harm… other powerful men."

Eleanor's eyes hardened. "And the rest?"

AJ stared at her.

"The rest," he said, "become lessons."

Harrington exhaled softly, as if AJ had finally spoken something long obvious.

Eleanor's jaw clenched.

"Then I need leverage," she said.

AJ blinked. "Leverage?"

Eleanor nodded slightly. "A name. A correspondence. A proof. Something that makes them fear me the way I fear them."

AJ felt his stomach drop.

She wasn't just asking for truth.

She was asking for ammunition.

And in a crisis, ammunition turns people into soldiers.

AJ looked toward Harrington instinctively, as if hoping Harrington would stop her.

Harrington did not move.

He simply said, quiet as a verdict:

"Miss Ashdown is correct."

Eleanor's gaze snapped to Harrington.

Harrington's voice was calm, bitter.

"Only leverage buys mercy," he said. "Not virtue."

Eleanor stared at him, then back at AJ.

"You see?" she said. "Even your chief clerk knows. Now—help me."

AJ's hands trembled slightly.

He thought of the statement he had signed—the official story that made Fordyce the single villain.

He thought of the ash he had crushed in his fist.

He thought of Scotland collapsing because London sneezed.

And he realized: he had already chosen sides once, when he signed.

Now he could choose again.

He lowered his voice.

"There is a ledger," AJ said. "An exposure ledger. With pencil marks."

Harrington's eyes tightened, but he did not stop him.

Eleanor's eyes flashed. "What kind of pencil marks?"

"Adjusted dates," AJ said. "Inflows made to look certain. Doubt erased in graphite."

Eleanor's face went still.

"That's fraud," she whispered.

Harrington's mouth tightened.

"It's… smoothing," Harrington said softly. "A desperate man's attempt to keep the machine calm."

Eleanor looked at Harrington sharply. "You call it smoothing," she said. "I call it lying."

Harrington's eyes held hers. "In a panic," he said, "everything is lying. Even calm."

Eleanor turned back to AJ. "Where is it?"

AJ hesitated. Then, because he could no longer bear half-truths, he answered.

"Locked in the back office," AJ said. "With other records."

Eleanor nodded, quick.

"Get it," she said.

AJ's throat tightened. "I can't just—"

Eleanor stepped closer, voice low. "Then you can watch people drown," she said. "And call it innocence."

The words stabbed.

AJ flinched.

He didn't want to be heroic.

He just didn't want to be useless.

He nodded once.

"I'll try," he said.

Eleanor exhaled. "Good."

She turned to go, then paused.

"And Mr. Sen?" she said.

AJ looked up.

Eleanor's eyes were fierce.

"If you help me," she said, "you will no longer be a clerk. You will be a participant."

AJ swallowed. "I already am," he said.

Eleanor's mouth tightened into something like respect.

Then she walked away into London's gray daylight, already calculating her next move.

THE RESCUE PATTERNS — LONDON

Later that day, Harrington sent AJ on errands that were not errands.

He was sent to deliver sealed packets to houses that still had their doors open.

One house received him with warmth and a quiet laugh.

"Ah," the senior partner said, "so the City breathes again, does it?"

AJ noticed the man's table.

On it lay a letter.

Not a panic letter. Not a demand.

A private note with Threadneedle Street's seal.

A smile.

An embrace.

Not for everyone.

AJ watched servants carry silver trays of tea through rooms filled with calm.

He thought: *So this is what being saved looks like.*

Then he visited another house, smaller, less connected.

The doors were half shut. The clerk inside looked hunted.

"Are you paying?" AJ asked quietly.

The clerk laughed once, bitter.

"Paying?" he said. "We are dying politely."

AJ left, stomach tight.

Outside, on the street, a crowd gathered—not at the great houses, but at the weaker ones.

Predators knew where to feed.

SCOTLAND — THE RUIN PATTERNS

In Scotland, the collapse was not only financial.

It was social.

Landowners who had treated the bank as an extension of their pride now sat at dinner tables staring at their wives, realizing their estates might be cut apart like meat.

Merchants who had extended credit to neighbors now demanded repayment like strangers.

A man named Gavin Reid—sheep-scented hands—returned home with no coin and a face that looked older.

His wife asked, "Did you get it?"

Gavin stared at the fire.

"No," he said.

And in that single syllable, a family's future shifted.

Rumor traveled through villages:

"Ayr Bank is finished."

"Heron is ruined."

"Douglas will sell land."

And with rumor came another pattern:

Some men found help.

Others were abandoned.

The ones with ties to Edinburgh, to English houses, to old family networks—those men received quiet accommodations, private notes, "temporary arrangements."

The rest received demands.

Ruin was not equal.

It was **allocated**.

AMSTERDAM — THE COST OF ICE

In Amsterdam, Jan van der Velde watched credit tighten like a noose.

He refused bills that would have been accepted a month ago.

He demanded hard settlement.

And each time he did, he saved himself a little—while starving someone else a lot.

A sugar merchant begged, voice trembling.

Jan shook his head.

"It's not personal," Jan said.

But it was personal.

Because personal was what happened when systems failed.

Jan's wife watched him at dinner and asked softly, "How many men will fail because of us?"

Jan's fork paused.

He didn't answer.

He couldn't.

Because to answer would be to accept he had become the kind of man he once despised.

THE BACK OFFICE — THE LEDGER

That evening, AJ returned to the bank after most clerks had left.

Harrington was still there, alone, sorting papers like a man arranging bones.

AJ approached carefully.

"I need the key," AJ said.

Harrington looked up slowly.

"To what?" he asked, though his eyes already knew.

AJ swallowed. "The back office. The ledger."

Harrington's expression tightened.

"Miss Ashdown," he murmured.

AJ nodded.

Harrington stared for a long moment.

Then he stood, opened a drawer, and removed a key.

He held it in his palm and looked at it as if it were a choice made physical.

"You think you're doing good," Harrington said quietly.

AJ's throat tightened. "I'm trying to do something."

Harrington's gaze was tired.

"Good," he said, "is a luxury. This is survival."

He placed the key in AJ's hand.

AJ closed his fingers around it.

The metal was cold.

Harrington's voice dropped.

"If you take that ledger," he said, "you do not simply expose a lie. You expose the men who needed the lie."

AJ swallowed. "I know."

Harrington's eyes held him.

"And those men," Harrington continued, "do not forgive."

AJ nodded once.

Harrington stepped back.

"Then go," Harrington said. "Before I change my mind."

AJ turned and moved down the corridor, heart hammering.

He reached the back office door.

The lock resisted for a moment, then yielded.

Inside, the room smelled of paper and dust and secrets.

Ledgers stacked on shelves.

Bundles of correspondence.

Boxes tied with twine.

This wasn't a room.

It was an archive of consequences.

AJ found the exposure ledger quickly—thick, worn, spine cracked.

He pulled it down.

His hands trembled.

He opened it.

There they were: the pencil marks.

Small adjustments that had tried to persuade reality to cooperate.

AJ shut the ledger and hugged it to his chest.

He turned.

And froze.

A figure stood in the doorway.

The stranger in the plain coat.

The "interests" man.

Watching.

AJ's blood went cold.

The man's gaze dropped to the ledger in AJ's arms.

Then lifted to AJ's face.

"You are working very late," the man said softly.

AJ's mouth went dry.

He could not lie fast enough.

The man stepped into the room.

Behind him, another man appeared—broader shoulders, quiet menace.

No uniforms.

No official papers.

Just power.

The plain-coat man smiled faintly.

"We offer safety," he said, voice mild.

"And you," he continued, "are attempting to purchase it elsewhere."

AJ's throat tightened.

He clutched the ledger tighter, as if paper could be armor.

The man's voice stayed calm.

"Who gets saved?" he asked, echoing Eleanor's question with cruel precision.

AJ's blood roared in his ears.

The man stepped closer.

"I'll tell you," he said softly.

"Those who understand," he whispered, "that the story belongs to us."

The broader man behind him shut the door.

The click of the latch sounded like a coffin closing.

AJ stood in the back office with the ledger in his arms, realizing he had just walked into the true center of the crisis:

Not money.

Not coin.

Not paper.

Control.

CHAPTER 10

THE WORLD ON CREDIT

The back office was quiet in the way a courtroom is quiet—because everyone understands that what happens next will be permanent.

AJ stood with the exposure ledger held tight against his chest, as if paper could stop a blade.

It couldn't.

The plain-coat man moved deeper into the room without urgency, like a man entering a property he already owned.

His companion—broad-shouldered, silent—stood near the door, blocking the only exit.

AJ's mouth went dry.

"What do you want?" AJ managed.

The plain-coat man tilted his head as if amused by the simplicity of the question.

"What we have always wanted," he said softly. "A controlled fire."

AJ's fingers tightened on the ledger. "People are ruined," he said. "Scotland is collapsing. Trade is freezing."

The man nodded, mild. "Yes," he said. "And it will freeze harder if the wrong truths leak at the wrong speed."

AJ stared. "Truth is truth."

The man's eyes softened, almost pitying.

"Truth," he said, "is timing."

He stepped closer.

"You are holding a document," he said, nodding toward the ledger, "that could create a second panic. A legal panic. A moral panic. A panic directed at the wrong targets."

AJ's throat tightened. "Wrong targets?" he whispered.

The man's smile was thin.

"The targets," he corrected, "we cannot afford to lose."

AJ swallowed hard.

"You want the ledger," AJ said.

The man didn't deny it. He extended his gloved hand.

"Give it to me," he said gently. "And you will remain safe."

AJ looked down at the ledger.

In those pages were pencil marks that made doubt look like certainty.

A small lie, repeated with calm handwriting.

And behind those pencil marks were men—partners, clerks, institutions—trying to survive.

AJ's mind flashed to Eleanor's face:

Only leverage buys mercy.

If AJ gave up the ledger, he lost leverage.

If he kept it, he might lose his life.

He looked up. "And if I don't?" AJ asked.

The broad-shouldered man shifted slightly.

The plain-coat man's voice remained mild.

"Then your name becomes useful," he said. "The city will find you very interesting."

AJ's stomach turned.

He could picture it: arrested, questioned, blamed. A clerk offered up like meat so the crowd could feel justice had occurred.

Fordyce gone. Partners protected. A young clerk crushed.

AJ's hands trembled.

Then, unexpectedly, a new sound entered the room.

Footsteps.

Fast.

Determined.

The door handle rattled.

The broad-shouldered man turned slightly, tightening his stance.

The door opened anyway.

Harrington stepped in.

His face was pale, but his eyes were clear.

He took in the scene at once: AJ cornered, the two men, the ledger.

Harrington's voice was calm.

"Gentlemen," he said, "you are in a private office."

The plain-coat man smiled faintly. "Mr. Harrington," he said. "Always industrious."

Harrington's jaw tightened. "Who are you?" Harrington asked.

The plain-coat man didn't answer directly.

"A concerned party," he said. "A friend of stability."

Harrington's gaze slid to AJ. "Leave," Harrington said quietly.

AJ blinked. "Sir—"

Harrington didn't look at him. "Now," he said, voice edged with command.

AJ hesitated.

Harrington finally looked at him, and in that look AJ saw something rare:

Care.

Not affection. Not tenderness.

But the recognition that a young man had been dragged into a machine that would not spare him.

"Go," Harrington said again.

AJ took a step toward the door.

The broad-shouldered man shifted to block him.

Harrington's voice sharpened. "Move," Harrington said.

The broad man smiled—just a fraction.

"We can't," he said.

Harrington stared. "Then you understand," Harrington said softly, "that if you harm him, you harm the story you're trying to control."

The plain-coat man's eyes narrowed slightly. "You think you have leverage," he said.

Harrington's smile was bleak. "I have reality," he replied.

He gestured at the shelves, the ledgers, the stacked papers.

"This bank is finished," Harrington said. "But the records remain. If you try to erase a truth, the act of erasing becomes louder than the truth itself."

The plain-coat man studied Harrington.

Then he sighed as if disappointed.

"Mr. Harrington," he said, "you are clever enough to understand the difference between destroying a ledger and destroying a rumor."

Harrington's eyes were hard. "And you are clever enough," Harrington replied, "to know that rumor is already loose."

The plain-coat man's gaze slid back to AJ.

"Give me the ledger," he said again.

AJ felt his heart pounding.

His hands tightened.

And in a moment that surprised even him, AJ spoke.

"You don't want the ledger," AJ said quietly.

The plain-coat man paused. "No?"

AJ's voice steadied, the way a man's voice sometimes steadies when fear becomes too large to contain.

"You want control," AJ said. "You want the story to stay simple."

The plain-coat man's smile returned. "Yes," he said. "That is control."

AJ swallowed.

"And if I give it to you," AJ continued, "you will still need someone to blame."

The plain-coat man didn't answer.

He didn't need to.

Silence is also a confession.

Harrington's jaw tightened. "He is correct," Harrington said.

The plain-coat man's mildness thinned into something colder.

"Mr. Sen," he said softly, "do not confuse insight with power."

AJ's fingers trembled on the ledger's spine.

He thought of Eleanor again—how she moved through men like she had learned that fear wastes time.

He thought of Scotland—men pounding doors, pride collapsing.

He thought of Amsterdam—merchant houses freezing credit, saving themselves by starving others.

And he thought of Fordyce, laughing as if reality were a toy.

I'm not afraid to short a god.

A god.

A system.

A belief.

The world.

AJ looked at the ledger and understood the final truth of the crisis:

This book was not merely evidence.

It was a **weapon**.

And weapons always demand a hand willing to use them.

AJ took a breath.

Then he did something that felt insane.

He opened the ledger.

The plain-coat man's eyes narrowed.

AJ flipped to the page with the most obvious pencil marks—the erased uncertainty, the adjusted inflow.

He held it up.

"This," AJ said, voice shaking but loud enough to carry, "is the lie."

The broad-shouldered man moved fast—

But Harrington stepped between them like a shield.

"Enough," Harrington snapped.

The plain-coat man held up a hand, stopping his companion.

He stared at AJ with a new kind of interest.

"You will show that," the man said softly, "to whom?"

AJ's throat tightened.

He didn't know.

Not really.

But then a voice answered from the doorway behind them.

A female voice.

Controlled. Cold.

"I will."

Eleanor Ashdown stood in the doorway.

She wore the same practical black coat, but her face was different now—harder, cleaner, like she had cut away her last illusions.

In her hand, she held something wrapped in cloth.

She stepped into the room without asking permission.

The broad-shouldered man's stance shifted toward her.

Eleanor's eyes flicked to him.

Then she unwrapped the cloth.

Not a pistol. Not a knife.

A stack of papers.

Receipts. Correspondence. Notes.

Names.

"You," Eleanor said, looking at the plain-coat man, "are not the only one who can collect a story."

The plain-coat man's mildness faltered. Just slightly.

Eleanor held up the papers.

"I have been trading," she said calmly, "in information. Since the moment you froze my credit."

She turned the top sheet toward Harrington and AJ.

"You want to know who gets saved?" Eleanor asked.

She pointed at a name.

"Men like this," she said.

AJ stared.

He recognized the seal.

Threadneedle Street's smiling letter.

An embrace.

The broad-shouldered man stepped forward.

Eleanor's gaze didn't move.

"If you touch me," she said quietly, "the papers go to the wrong hands by morning."

The broad-shouldered man froze.

Because she was telling the truth.

Eleanor looked at AJ.

"Give me the ledger," she said.

AJ's hands tightened.

The plain-coat man's voice was very soft now.

"Miss Ashdown," he said, "you are making a mistake."

Eleanor smiled faintly. "No," she said. "I'm making a trade."

She stepped closer to AJ.

Her eyes held his.

"Mr. Sen," she said, "you wanted to rise. This is how you rise."

AJ swallowed. "By burning the world?"

Eleanor's face didn't soften.

"The world is already burning," she said. "I'm deciding where the flame goes."

AJ looked at Harrington.

Harrington's eyes were tired, but clear.

Harrington nodded once—small, almost invisible.

A permission.

Or forgiveness.

AJ handed Eleanor the ledger.

Eleanor took it as if receiving a sword.

The plain-coat man's smile vanished completely.

"This is unwise," he said.

Eleanor didn't look at him.

"You will offer accommodation," she said calmly. "To my creditors. To my warehouse. You will thaw the ice you created."

The plain-coat man's voice was quiet. "You are blackmailing—"

"I am negotiating," Eleanor corrected. "Like you."

She turned her gaze to the broad-shouldered man.

"And you," she said, "will open the door."

The man hesitated.

Then, slowly, he moved.

The door opened.

Air rushed in like freedom.

Eleanor looked at AJ one last time.

"You can come with me," she said. "Or you can stay here and be managed."

AJ's heart pounded.

To go with her meant stepping fully into the machinery.

To stay meant being crushed by it.

He stepped toward Eleanor.

Harrington's voice stopped him.

"Sen," Harrington said softly.

AJ turned.

Harrington's eyes held his.

"Remember," Harrington said, "that every crisis is the same story with a new costume."

AJ swallowed. "Yes, sir."

Harrington's mouth tightened into something like a smile.

"Then write it," Harrington said.

AJ turned and left with Eleanor.

The plain-coat man watched them go, face unreadable.

As the door shut behind them, he murmured to his companion:

"Find another clerk."

EPILOGUE IMAGE — THE WORLD ON CREDIT

That night, AJ stood by his window above the bakery, staring at the city.

London's lamps glowed like scattered embers.

The crisis was not over.

It would spread, reshape, scar.

But a story was already forming—one that would be told in Parliament, in coffeehouses, in courtrooms, in future books.

A simple villain.

A contained fire.

A lesson.

AJ held a single object in his hand:

A small bill of exchange, worthless now, ink fading at the edges.

A promise that had once moved ships.

He turned it over and saw the signature.

A flourish.

A confident hand.

A man who had believed he could outrun consequences.

AJ whispered, almost to himself:

"The world doesn't run on gold."

He watched the paper tremble in his fingers.

"It runs on belief," he continued. "And belief runs on stories."

He folded the bill slowly—carefully—like folding a flag.

And as he did, a thought settled in him with terrifying clarity:

This was not the first time credit had lied.

It would not be the last.

Somewhere in the city, men were already building the next instrument, the next promise, the next elegant way to sell tomorrow.

AJ looked out at London's lights and understood what his life had become:

A witness.

A pen.

A participant.

And he knew, with certainty.

When the world lives on credit, every generation invents a new way to repeat the same sin.

END OF 1772: The First Credit Panic

www.ingramcontent.com/pod-product-compliance
Ingram Content Group UK Ltd.
Pitfield, Milton Keynes, MK11 3LW, UK
UKHW021407190726
13845UKWH00028B/937